THEORY AND PRACTICE

THE SEMINARS OF JACQUES DERRIDA

Edited by Geoffrey Bennington & Peggy Kamuf

Theory and Practice

Jacques Derrida

Translated by David Wills

Edited by Geoffrey Bennington and Peggy Kamuf

The University of Chicago Press ‡ CHICAGO AND LONDON

The University of Chicago Press, Chicago 60637
The University of Chicago Press, Ltd., London
© 2019 by The University of Chicago
All rights reserved. No part of this book may be used or reproduced in any manner whatsoever without written permission, except in the case of brief quotations in critical articles and reviews. For more information, contact the University of Chicago Press, 1427 E. 60th St., Chicago, IL 60637.
Published 2019
Paperback edition 2024
Printed in the United States of America

33 32 31 30 29 28 27 26 25 24   1 2 3 4 5

ISBN: 978-0-226-57234-5 (cloth)
ISBN: 978-0-226-82935-7 (paper)
ISBN: 978-0-226-57248-2 (e-book)
DOI: https://doi.org/10.7208/chicago/9780226572482.001.0001

Originally published as *Théorie et pratique* © 2017 Éditions Galilée.

Library of Congress Cataloging-in-Publication Data

Names: Derrida, Jacques, author. | Wills, David, 1953– translator. | Derrida, Jacques. Works. Selections. English. 2009.
Title: Theory and practice / Jacques Derrida ; translated by David Wills.
Other titles: Théorie et pratique. English
Description: Chicago : The University of Chicago Press, 2018. |
Series: The seminars of Jacques Derrida
Identifiers: LCCN 2018023877 | ISBN 9780226572345 (cloth : alk. paper) | ISBN 9780226572482 (e-book)
Subjects: LCSH: Theory (Philosophy) | Practice (Philosophy) | Philosophy, Marxist.
Classification: LCC B842 .D4713 2018 | DDC 194—dc23
LC record available at https://lccn.loc.gov/2018023877

CONTENTS

Foreword to the English Edition : vii
General Introduction to the French Edition : ix
Translator's Preface : xiii

FIRST SESSION : 1

SECOND SESSION : 19

THIRD SESSION : 39

FOURTH SESSION : 53

FIFTH SESSION : 69

SIXTH SESSION : 83

SEVENTH SESSION : 97

EIGHTH SESSION : 107

NINTH SESSION : 117

Index of Names : 127

FOREWORD TO THE ENGLISH EDITION

The French edition of *Théorie et pratique* (Paris: Galilée, 2017) marks a departure in several respects from the editorial policies and practices developed over the previous ten years for the publication of Derrida's seminars. As Alexander García Düttmann makes explicit in his introduction to that edition, he has made a large number of "silent" corrections to Derrida's typescript, including reordering or rewriting sentences he judges to be incomplete or otherwise incoherent, changing Derrida's use of punctuation and capitalization, and eliminating Derrida's characteristic use of what in French we have come to call *reprises*—that is, repetition for clarity of the beginning of a sentence after an aside or digression. In practice, this means that significant editorial interventions, invisible to the reader, have been made on every page of the French volume. Düttmann also introduces several errors or inaccuracies into the text, most notably misidentifying the year of this seminar as 1975–76 (in fact it dates from the following year), and adds some interpretative footnotes that go beyond editorial concerns.

As members of the original editorial team responsible for editing the French volumes of the seminar, and as general editors of the English translations, we have preferred to maintain the original editorial policies and practices. Consequently, the translation presented here is based not on the published French edition, but directly on the typescript of the seminar itself, the original of which is found in the Critical Theory Archive at the University of California, Irvine. This means that David Wills has translated the text that Derrida actually wrote, with only minimal editorial interventions in conformity with previous publications in this series. We also reinstate here the "General Introduction to the French Edition," and do not translate Düttmann's editorial note, which largely discusses his departures, not followed in this edition, from previous editorial practice.

Geoffrey Bennington
Peggy Kamuf
JANUARY 2018

GENERAL INTRODUCTION TO THE
FRENCH EDITION

The complete edition of Jacques Derrida's seminars and lectures will give the reader the chance of an unprecedented contact with the philosopher's teaching voice. This edition will constitute a new part of his oeuvre, to be distinguished from the books and other texts published during his lifetime or revised by him before his death, and with a clearly different status. It is not certain that Jacques Derrida would have published the seminars as they stand: probably he would have reorganized or rewritten them. Taken as a whole, but also in their relation to Derrida's philosophical oeuvre, these lectures and seminars will constitute an incomparable research tool and will, we believe, give a different experience of his thinking, here linked to his teaching, which was always, both in France and abroad, a truly vital resource of his writing.

The corpus we are preparing for publication is vast. From the beginning of his teaching career, Derrida was in the habit of completely writing out almost all his lectures and seminars. This means that we have at our disposal the equivalent of some fourteen thousand printed pages, or forty-three volumes, on the basis of one volume per academic year. This material can be classified according to a variety of criteria. First, according to the place where the teaching took place: the Sorbonne from 1960 to 1964; the École normale supérieure in the rue d'Ulm, from 1964 to 1984; the École des hautes études en sciences sociales (EHESS) from 1984 to 2003.[1] Then

---

1. We need to add the American places as well: from fall 1968 to 1974 at the Johns Hopkins University, then as visiting professor in the humanities from 1975 to 1986 at Yale University, where he gave each year, in the fall or spring semester, a regular seminar. From 1987 to 2003, Derrida taught regularly at the University of California, Irvine, and at the New School for Social Research, the Cardozo Law School, and New York University (1992–2003). This American teaching (which, with a few exceptions,

according to the type of teaching: classes with a very variable number of sessions (from one to fifteen) up until 1964; what he always called "seminars" thereafter. Finally—and no doubt most relevantly for the editorial work—according to the tools used: we have handwritten sessions from 1960 to 1970; typescripts, with manuscript annotations and corrections, from 1970 to 1988; electronic files and printouts from 1988 to 2003.

Derrida's seminars, which already had their own style and already attracted a broad and numerous following at the rue d'Ulm (where the choice of subjects and authors, if not the way they were treated, was constrained by the program of the Agrégation),[2] take on their definitive character at the EHESS where, on Wednesdays from 5 p.m. to 7 p.m., a dozen times a year, Jacques Derrida, sometimes improvising a little, would read before a large audience the text of his seminar, entirely written out for each session as the year proceeded. (Add to that a few improvised sessions, sometimes around a reading, and a few discussion sessions.) Henceforth free in his choice of subjects, Derrida launched research projects over periods of several years, which link together in explicit, coherent, and gripping fashion. The great question of philosophical nationality and nationalism (1984–88) leads to that of the "Politics of Friendship" (1988–91), and then to the long series of "Questions of Responsibility" (1991–2003), focusing successively on the Secret (1991–92), Testimony (1992–95), Hostility and Hospitality (1995–97), Perjury and Pardon (1997–99) and the Death Penalty (1999–2001), with the final two years devoted to "The Beast and the Sovereign" (2001–3).

Derrida was in the habit of drawing on the abundant material of these seminars for the very numerous lectures he gave every year throughout the world, and often, via this route, parts of the seminars were reworked and published. Several of his books also find their point of departure in the work of the seminar: *Of Grammatology* (1967), for example, in large part develops sessions of the 1965–66 seminar on "Nature, Culture, Writing"; the seminar on "Hegel's Family" (1971–72) is picked up in *Glas* (1974). *Politics of Friendship* (1994) is explicitly presented as the expansion of the first session of the 1988–89 seminar, and there are traces in it of other sessions too. But in spite of these partial convergences and correspondences, the vast majority of the

---

repeated the EHESS seminar) was given at first in French, but after 1987 most often in English: Derrida would improvise during the session an English version of his text, which he had previously annotated for this purpose.

2. [Translator's Note]: The Agrégation is the notoriously competitive qualifying examination taken by prospective higher-level teachers in the secondary and university systems.

pages written from week to week for the seminar remain unpublished and will incomparably complement the work already published. Whenever a session was later published by Jacques Derrida, in modified form or not, we will give the reference. We do not consider it appropriate for the edition of the seminars themselves, as original material, to offer a comparative reading of those versions.

As we have already pointed out, the editorial work varies considerably according to the mode of production of the text. For the typewriter period, many handwritten amendments and annotations require a considerable effort of decipherment; the more so for the seminars entirely written in Derrida's handsome but difficult handwriting, which require laborious transcription. So we shall begin by publishing the seminars of the last twenty years, while beginning preparation of the rest. In all cases, our primary goal is to present the *text* of the seminar, as *written* by Derrida, *with a view to* speech, to reading aloud, and thus with some marks of anticipated orality and some familiar turns of phrase. It is not certain that Derrida would have published these seminars, although he occasionally expressed his intention of doing so,[3] but if he had taken up these texts for publication, he would probably have reworked them, as he always did, in the direction of a more written text. Obviously we have not taken it upon ourselves to do that work in his place. As we mentioned above, the reader may wish to compare the original version presented here with the few sessions published separately by Jacques Derrida himself.

Geoffrey Bennington
Marc Crépon
Marguerite Derrida
Thomas Dutoit
Peggy Kamuf
Michel Lisse
Marie-Louise Mallet
Ginette Michaud

---

3. See, for example, the foreword to *Politiques de l'amitié* (Paris: Galilée, 1994), p. 11; *Politics of Friendship*, trans. George Collins (London: Verso Books, 1997), p. vii.

TRANSLATOR'S PREFACE

Theory and Practice is the translation of a seminar Derrida held at the École Normale Supérieure during the 1976–77 academic year. Its title derives from the subject imposed nationally for students preparing for the *agrégation* examination. As the reader of these sessions will come to see, the particular interest of this series is at least twofold. First, the seminar begins from Marx's "Theses on Feuerbach," particularly the 11th Thesis, and develops a discussion of the Marxist understanding of practice in the context of philosophical interpretations elaborated, especially by Derrida's colleague Louis Althusser, during the preceding decade. Those interpretations were still very much common currency in 1976–77, and part of a very politically charged atmosphere in the period following 1968 (Derrida had already alluded to aspects of the Marxist concept of "production" vis-à-vis "reproduction," in his previous year's seminar, "Life Death"). *Theory and Practice* can therefore be said to fill, to some extent, the long hiatus widely thought to exist in Derrida's treating of Marx between his call for a deconstructive reading in *Positions* (1972) and the later *Specters of Marx* (1993).

The second striking interest of *Theory and Practice* is in the way Derrida moves from practice, through *praxis*, to *technē*, which allows him to recast the topic in the light of Heidegger's "Question Concerning Technology," and to provide the only serious sustained analysis of that essay known to exist in his writings, even though, as is now clear, technics was always for him—but perhaps increasingly so from this point on—the site of a major articulation connecting his own work to that of the German philosopher.

The initial focus, or motor, of the seminar is the French expression *(il) faut le faire*, which in contemporary English parlance has something of the force of the slogan "let's (just) do it," as well as a series of other digressive senses that are developed through the discussion (see, to begin, my footnote in the "First Session"). Obviously there is resistance, and irony, in Derrida's reaction to the topic "Theory and Practice," to the presumed opposition of its terms (similar resistance to the topic "Life and Death" had been expressed a year earlier), and to the presumed political sense of that opposition; to the idea that there is *thinking* on one side and *doing* on the other, and that any revolutionary changing of the world is necessarily on the side of *doing*. He therefore sets about making "doing" a highly problematized undertaking, a problematization that proceeds by colloquializing the term, which is *practiced* at the outset in its informal, popular form, *faut le faire*.

For reasons explained in the "Foreword to the English Edition," this is a translation of the typescript of Derrida's seminar rather than of the published French version. This means that on occasion I have had to make editorial decisions where the typescript presents difficulties (typographical errors, handwritten marginal or interlinear additions, incomplete sentences, and so on). These decisions have been made in consultation with the series general editors on the basis of the policies developed for earlier publications of Derrida's seminars, policies that the editor of the French volume elected not to follow. I am nevertheless grateful to Alexander García Düttmann for his editorial labors, and especially for identifying references and adding clarifications that I have, in many cases, retained in the text.

The policies just referred to call for "silent" editorial correction only of obvious typographical slips and for insertion into the main text of marginal or interlinear additions only where their place is clearly marked in the typescript. All other changes are signaled in the text by the use of <angle brackets> around words supplied editorially, and in additional translator's notes clearly indicated as such.

This translation has benefited enormously from the corrections and suggestions made by colleagues and graduate student participants in the Derrida Seminars Translation Project workshop held at the IMEC (Institut Mémoire de l'Édition Contemporaine) in July 2016. I am therefore profoundly grateful to my fellow team members: Geoffrey Bennington, Pascale-Anne Brault, Peggy Kamuf, Michael Naas, and Elizabeth Rottenberg; to Ellen Burt, Katie Chenoweth, and Kir Kuiken; and to Ellie Anderson, Ernesto Blanes, Phil Lynes, David Maruzzella, Michael Peterson, Brigitte Stepanov, and Dashiell Wasserman. I wish also to thank Rodrigo Therezo for his kind help in locating certain references in the Library of Jacques Derrida, Studio Series, at the Princeton University Library.

FIRST SESSION

Theory and practice, then.

(It) must be done [*Faut le faire*].[1]

When I say *faut le faire*, what am I doing?

Of course, or so it would seem, I am heaving a sigh of discouragement, discouragement tinged with ironic protest at the curriculum that requires us to deal, in one year and in the form of a seminar, with such a question, if that is what it is. As I do each year—but rest assured I won't take it beyond this year—I'll start by critically analyzing the situation that is imposed on us by inviting you not to be satisfied with critiquing it, in theory, but to try to transform this situation effectively, practically. No further in that direction.

But if you analyze the sigh that I let slip in a little more rigorously, if you analyze it beyond the sense of disappointed fatigue on my part that it may convey, beyond my admission of impotence and my refusal to deal with such a subject in these forms, if you consider the ready-made expression *faut le faire*, I say if you consider it, whereas you precisely cannot consider it, you can only understand it in a given situation, that is to say determined as an event, in a context. And according to the context, a context of a particular type, for there are types of context, and contextual variability is not absolutely empirical and atypical, it includes possibilities for regulation on the basis of type, if then you understand it in a context of a particular type there are at least two senses[2] to the locution *faut le faire* in our language. It either means:

---

1. [Translator's Note]: As explained in the preface, this expression will become something of a motto for the seminar. It is a contraction of *il faut le faire*, literally "it is necessary to do it." Besides various informal versions of that literal sense, the expression also functions as an expletive ("takes some doing!"), registering surprise or shock that someone would have the nerve or temerity to do something. Derrida plays on that usage below.

2. [Translator's Note]: The word "senses" is circled by hand and linked to two marginal additions: "2 emphases [*accentuations*], 2 dimensions [*portées*]."

First emphasis; it will keep us here for quite some time.

1. It is not enough to talk about it, or to promise, or consider, look at, hear, or receive it passively, to talk about it, or think of it, it must be done, in other words there "must be practice." Theory is not enough, there must be practice. But you can already see the difficulty of doing—a difficulty connoted by the expression *faut le faire*, which always means "it's not easy" because it isn't enough to consider, look, hear, wait for, receive passively, be content to talk about it or think of it or intend it—it still must be done and that's more difficult, that's what is difficult. But this difficulty, though, is not only what is directly uttered by what I say when I say *faut le faire*, it is already within the difficulty of understanding (thinking, understanding, determining, considering) what I mean when I say *faut le faire*. You have seen—or heard—that even before knowing what doing [*faire*] means one knew that its sense, its meaning-to-say would be determined only in the context of an opposition: doing as opposed here to thinking, representing, there to looking, considering, or again to speaking, saying, and even in opposition to several sorts of saying, of language, language uttering what is or language uttering what will be, and what will be in the form of theoretical expectation *or else* in the form of a commitment or promise. "I am going to do it": it isn't enough to say I am going to do it, it must be done; but *I am going to do it* can itself be an expectation or a commitment; in saying I am going to do it, this seminar, I may be announcing that doing it is within what I can foresee, that it is merely to come, but I may also be announcing that I commit to doing it, by means of a promise and a contract. And even, added complication, saying that I intend to do it does not signify that I promise to do it; it's not the same thing, the same sense, the same intention, such that the utterance "I am going" to do it can signify a theoretical expectation, either an intention without commitment or promise, or else a promise. And one could still refine things much more, as we will no doubt do later. For the moment I am content to register that the "doing" of "must be done" includes, in addition to the difficulty that it states ("must be done"), the difficulty of understanding what it does in saying "must be done," doing being determined solely within an opposition; and to be opposite to thinking is not to be opposite to representing, or to looking, or speaking or saying, or expecting or promising, or being passive. Each time, in each instance of the opposition, *doing* signifies something else, and sometimes something else entirely. Not only does it signify something else according to whether it is opposed to thinking, or knowing, speaking, expecting, promising, etc., but it can on occasion signify one of those opposites opposed to another one. It is not enough to think it, it must be said, where saying comes down to doing,

it is not enough to intend to promise, it must be promised where promising consists in doing, acting, producing, transforming, therefore, wherever there was only mute thinking or interior discourse or discourse that was theoretical, constative, <illegible handwritten word>, etc. That is in order to announce, in a somewhat jumbled way, the immense difficulty that lies before us, as a theoretical problem and/or practical task. For if one must know what is meant by thinking, representing, speaking, saying, intending, theorizing, speculating, promising, etc., in order to know what doing means, then we won't be able to avoid dealing with an enormous history that cannot be only a history of meaning or a semantico-philosophical one.

When I said that "must be done" determines its *doing* only by reference to an opposite, in the oppositional situation that places it in respect of X Y Z (thinking, saying, wanting to, intending, claiming, expecting, promising), I myself seemed to imply, given our context, itself determined by the program "theory-practice," not only that the word "theory" can, in decisive contexts, cover this or that point along the chain "think, say, want to, intend, speculate, promise," but more precipitately still I seemed to presume that *doing* <=> *practice*.³ Yet nothing is less simple and less evident. The semantic value of what is practical [*du pratique*] or of practice, indeed of *praxis*, supposing—this is purely hypothetical for the moment—it to be unifiable, such a semantic value cannot be accounted for simply by what one calls *doing*, even supposing that value of *doing* to be itself unifiable. Just as what is theoretical about theory can play along a scale [*clavier*] that goes from *theorein* as gazing, or (not the same thing) contemplating (privileging, as is all too easy today to state, or make of an affair of state [*d'en faire état, ou affaire d'état*], the metaphor of the gaze), well then, just as the theoretical can play along a scale going from the powerful optical or eidetic metaphor all the way to thinking, cognizance, knowledge, <illegible handwritten word>, discourse, language, science as opposed to action, intention as opposed to action, etc., so practice can play along a semantic scale going from the very rich semantic hub of the Greek *praxis*, already very enigmatic (as we'll see), all the way to values such as act, action, gesture (gaze?), transformation, operation, effectuation, execution, labor, production, technique (*technē* no doubt playing a very important role in this semantic history), etc.⁴

---

3. [Translator's Note]: The typescript has a colon between *faire* and *pratique*; it is taken here to represent "=."

4. [Translator's Note]: Throughout this volume *technique* will be systematically transliterated as "technique" even though, in many cases, more recent English usage might favor "technics," "technicity," or "technology." That choice is justified by the fact

If one takes into account the fact that these two—what I have just more or less blithely called "these two"—scales combine their oppositions, one finds oneself dealing with a very complex oppositional machine and semantic network [*combinatoire*]. Confronted with such a machine, within it rather, since we have no absolute remove from this semantico-linguistic element within which, in any case, we are, what must we do [*que devons-nous faire*]?[5]

I note to begin that "what must we do" already presents itself as a task and duty, as the question deliberating over a task or duty that one would have to fulfill. The question I posed was not "are we going to do something?" since it is understood that it must be done, but *what* to do, what are we going to do? What is the content of what must be done, confronted with this machine, within it rather? I'll come back to this "must [*il faut*]."

There are two types of possibility here, of possible responses among which, it seems, we would have to choose. Before defining summarily these two types, I'll first put aside, I'll distance myself from a path that could be legitimate but along which I'd surely get bored myself and probably you also: this is the path that we took last year regarding *life death*,[6] a path that led us to call into question in general terms, and through several problematic corpora or fields, the oppositional logic (dialectical or not) that, by means of the *and*, related death and life one to the other. Deconstructing the oppositional (that is to say philosophical) logic in the case of "theory and practice" would also be possible and necessary, as in the case of this rule concerning philosophy curricula that always proposes an opposition, a position or apposition, to be thought through. But the principle of this deconstruction having been already set out and exemplified, we are not going to start again with another example.

I was saying, then: two possibilities: the first, more genealogical in appearance, would consist essentially in a semantic, indeed etymological exploration. What does "theoretical" mean? what does "practical" mean? and

---

that Derrida does not show any discomfort with the word, and seems prepared, once he comes to discuss Heidegger's "Die Frage nach der Technik," to allow the French transliteration of German *Technik* to stand, presumably in order to preserve its link to Greek *tekhnē*. The standard English translation of Heidegger's essay of course chooses "technology."

5. [Translator's Note]: Derrida's earlier impersonal formulation [*il faut le faire*] is here modified [*que devons-nous faire?*] by use of the verb *devoir*, which plays rather on senses of duty and obligation.

6. [Translator's Note]: Derrida's title for the previous year's seminar—in response to the prescribed agrégation topic, "Life and Death"—was "Life Death."

how is their oppositional relation established? One might consult dictionaries, everyday language, a family of everyday languages, *the* family of everyday languages, natural languages within which philosophical and scientific discourse coheres and is determined, that is Greek in the first instance (since theory and practice are Greek words, of Greek origin, as one says, in spite of what may have happened to them subsequently), then Latin (*contemplatio/ actio*, etc.), then German (*betrachten/wirken* for example, to isolate these elements within their arborescence), French, Franco-Latin (*contempler, spéculer/ agir, effectuer*, etc.).

This arborescent genealogy is of course very complex. It seems to pass through reference points of a textual type, in the classic sense of the word "text," and even to privilege philosophical textual references, references internal or presumed to be internal to the philosophical tradition, to what one presumes to be the unity or systemic immanence of something like the history of philosophy, to which one can if one wishes add "Western."

I am going to give some examples; very quickly, very summarily, on an indicative basis only, and we will need to take up this task again later in a more patient manner. If we were to look *today* for the *specifically philosophical* field in which the theory/practice opposition remains active, invested, deemed useful, pertinent, it would indeed seem to be within a philosophical discourse of the Marxian or Marxist tradition, or in any case marked by that tradition, reckoning with it, importing what, in such a tradition, has imbued the theory/practice pair with conceptual determinations. I won't say that that opposition is invested only in this Marxist place, or in contact with Marxism, but that it is only in such a place that it takes a philosophical form—at first sight at least—which is given to it in a regulated and systematic way by dialectical materialism. We would therefore start out from that place, here, today, with the aim of developing a semantico-philosophical genealogy, and leave aside either as irrelevant from this point of view, or as secondary, recourse that might be had to the theory/practice pair in everyday language, in empirico-approximate language, which fails to think rigorously, that is to say conceptually (theoretically?), what it says, or the recourse that might be had to it in domains such as those of science, I mean of a determinate science, regional sciences, where the theory/practice opposition is able to intervene in frequent and necessary ways, not only in all the classic problems of theory and experiment, all the epistemological problems concerning experimentation, or induction, or technical equipment, etc., but also in the problems that arise between the body of scientific research determined as theoretico-technical and the field of political practice, politico-economic practice (questions concerning the directions taken by research, concerning funding, equipment, ministries of science, international collaboration, the utilization of scientific research for peaceful or non-peaceful ends, in short the whole enormous and fundamental problem of the "politics of science" and of the political status of scientific theory). All of that would be left aside as not specifically philosophical or in any case as derivative, dependent vis-à-vis a philosophical determination of the theory/practice problem. In the same way, for example, the problematic topos of psychoanalysis would also be left aside: what is a theory for psychoanalysis, what is psychoanalytic theory, what specific relations exist between practice and theory in psychoanalysis? What is specific to psychoanalytic practice? And within the treatment, what is it that gets called "acting out," etc.? In the same way we would leave aside as something regional, concerning ordinary linguistic usage, the whole problematic—let's call it Anglo-Saxon—of the performative and of speech acts,[7] that is to say not the practical consequences of every sort that a theoretical language can have (this already constitutes an enormous and complex problematic field: what are the effects, psychic, political, pedagogical, etc., etc., of a discourse that in itself gives the appearance of being theoretical, that says what is), not only, therefore, the problem of the consequences or else of the practical causes that a theoretical discourse can have, but also, in a more acute manner, what a discourse of this or that type *does* (for example the type that Austin has in mind when he uses the name "performative") when it consists in doing, when it is in itself an act, such as when I say—these are now routine examples—"I open this session," "I name you knight of the Legion of Honor," "I commit to doing this or that," utterances that don't describe anything, that provide nothing that can be stated or known but do something and constitute events. According to the hypothesis of a rigorously philosophical genealogy that I am provisionally advancing for the moment, the problematic of the performative and of speech acts (to which we will naturally have to return) would be kept aside and considered derivative. Naturally these three examples (the epistemological, let's say, psychoanalytic, and logico-analytical) could be multiplied, almost without limit. Each time that a domain, a region, a place gets determined (pedagogy, medicine, sport, etc.), a theory/practice question gets determined, and the philosopher, whatever interest or importance he gives to it, considers it derivative, regional, dependent, and he basically reasons in the following way: one must first appeal to the most general, the most fundamental conceptual determination of the theory/practice pair, and know first how things stand with theory/practice in general in order to know next how things stand in these particular

---

7. [Translator's Note]: Here, and below, "speech acts" is in English in the typescript.

areas. Basically it is fundamental as such for the philosopher to know (and eventually to teach specialists) what "theory-and-practice" means in general, the sense of that opposition in general such as it is consistently presupposed in the regional fields that I just mentioned. Whatever the specificity of those usages, as much in epistemology as in psychoanalysis or in the problematic of speech acts and of the performative, they must all gesture toward a common and minimal semantic kernel, toward an implicit philosopheme that the philosopher himself, or philosophical discourse treats as such. Now, I was saying, therefore, that from that point of view, today, in "modern times," the philosophical discourse that takes under its aegis in an invested way the theory/practice pair, making it a major motif of its discursivity, is the discourse of a Marxist tradition, more precisely dialectical materialist philosophy. That is hard to dispute, I think, whatever the complexity, indeed novelty (we'll have to come back to all of this, of course) of the treatment of this pair in Marxist discourse, or rather Marxist discourses. Given that fact, the semantico-philosophical genealogy that we are talking about could, for example, go back from a certain current state of Marxist discourse on theory/practice to an "event" (I'll keep this word very indeterminate for the moment), a theoretical or practical event—whether it is theoretical or practical can be said only on the basis of the (theoretical or practical, etc.) interpretation of the relations between theory and practice—an event to be conceived either as crux, or as displacement, or as break, an event within which there is constituted something like Marxist discourse or rather, shall we say, theory/practice, Marxist theory/practice *qua philosophy*, as the philosophical system otherwise called dialectical materialism. All the important questions of this type: is Marxism or dialectical materialism a philosophy? is there or must there be a Marxist philosophy (and in that case what does philosophy mean?), or, adopting the formula that was recently proposed, is there merely a "Marxist status" of philosophy? does Marxism gain or lose by being presented, or by still presenting itself as a philosophy, and in what sense? All these important and difficult questions clearly lie on the horizon of this seminar. But for the moment, in this barely preliminary introduction, I'll be satisfied with marking some points of reference to justify finding my point of departure in current Marxist discourse or in the present state of "dialectical materialism" *qua philosophy*, as philosophical movement having as its indispensable basis the theory/practice pair and putting into perspective from its own philosophical position the whole history of philosophy and the whole history of the theory/practice pair. The two reference points that I would choose (but there could probably be others: whether they would be more pertinent or not, whether they would contribute something essentially new or different to the demonstration, I don't think so and that's why I limit myself to these ones, but I am ready to examine any other proposition, of course), the two reference points that I would choose belong to two discourses that have at least this much in common, failing all else, and have it in common with every Marxist discourse, namely that they always refer—as the historical, theoretical and practical reference—to this event, which I won't be able to qualify differently (what must it be called, what qualifier should it be given: theoretical, practical, philosophical or more than philosophical, etc.), this event, then, called "Theses on Feuerbach," and notably the 11th Thesis: *Die Philosophen haben die Welt nur verschieden* interpretiert, *es kommt darauf an, sie zu* verändern, which is generally translated as "Philosophers have only *interpreted* the world, in various ways; what is important is to transform it [*verändern*: to change, to make other, rather than transform, presuming one wants to keep for the concept of transformation—change in form, or change of the form, with all that that implies—a relevance that is more rigorous]."[8]

For our part, relying on a style that is perhaps not that of current Marxist problematics, we'll have cause to question the status of this utterance differently, and to accentuate it, accentuate it in several ways, to analyze in particular *es kommt darauf an*, difficult to translate, since "what is important" renders only one dimension of the expression, even if that dimension is, precisely, important. And still, one must understand fully what "important" means, understand fully the "must be done" implied by it, but how is one to understand a "must be done," "would have to be done": *es kommt*—what type of utterance is that? How is it to be understood, by analyzing the utterance, by seeking for it a sense or a referent (but by definition it doesn't yet have any), or by doing it, etc.?[9]

What is noteworthy, in any case, is that despite its aphoristic character, struck like a medal, the 11th Thesis comes to be determined only within a vast context; and it is difficult to miss the fact that in its most immediate context, namely that of the ten preceding theses—let's not forget that these

---

8. [Translator's Note]: Transliteration of the French translation to which Derrida refers (Karl Marx, "Thèses sur Feuerbach," in *L'Idéologie allemande*, by Friedrich Engels and Karl Marx, trans. R. Cartelle and G. Badia [Paris: Éditions Sociales, 1965], 98). Cf. "The philosophers have only *interpreted* the world, in various ways; the point is to *change* it" (Karl Marx, "Theses on Feuerbach," in *The German Ideology*, by Karl Marx and Friedrich Engels, pt. 1, ed. C. J. Arthur [New York: International Publishers, 1970]), 123. The following handwritten marginal addition accompanies this quotation: "practice → change (other) / transform <4–5 illegible words>."

9. [Translator's Note]: A handwritten marginal addition appears near the bottom of this paragraph: "Is it a matter of necessity?"

are *theses* but let's not be too quick to understand what *thesis* means here: for three reasons each of a different order:[10]

1. thesis = philosophy (neither literary, nor scientific);
2. in fact the title "Theses on Feuerbach" is not Marx's, but was assigned by the Moscow Institute for Marxism-Leninism at the time of the first edition of *German Ideology* in 1932, but that institute did so by referring to Engels, who precisely defined this brief text, a sketch that wasn't intended for publication, precisely as "theses," it's in the preface to his *Ludwig Feuerbach and the End of Classical German Philosophy* (1886): "In an old notebook of Marx's I have found the eleven theses on Feuerbach.... These are notes hurriedly scribbled down for later elaboration, absolutely not intended for publication, but invaluable as the first document in which is deposited the brilliant germ of the new world outlook."[11] That definition and the future destiny of this text in world history transfer their powerful enigma, and their power as enigma and as a very unusual textual event onto the concept of *text* (if this document is indeed a text) and onto the theory/practice pair, if, as we shall see, it constitutes the cornerstone of these 11 theses.
3. perhaps the thetic character of these theses comes to be determined only in close relation to what is uttered here, namely "what is important" (*es kommt darauf*: it would be necessary, it would have to be done, the thesis posing not a meaning, a truth, a theorem but a certain type of practical imperative or imperative performative: command, wish, *telos*, rallying cry [*mot d'ordre*], must be done.[12] We'll perhaps try to explain together later on the Anglo-Saxon logico-analytical problematic of speech acts and of the performative, in conjunction with certain themes that are quite foreign to it: the political slogan, position-taking in philosophy, and all non-constative, non-descriptive discourses). As I was saying, then,

---

10. [Translator's Note]: This phrase, and the numbering that follows, is determined by this handwritten marginal insertion: "For 3 reasons each of a different order: 1. thesis = φ (neither literary nor scientific); 2. Cf. p. 9a [addition on following page of typescript]; 3. → ." That apparent sequence has been followed here.

11. Friedrich Engels, *Ludwig Feuerbach and the End of Classical German Philosophy* (Moscow: Progress Publishers, 1969), 6.

12. [Translator's Note]: A handwritten marginal addition here appears to state: "I don't oppose what Althusser is doing <illegible parenthesis>, slogan [*mot d'ordre*] and concept. Read Alt<husser> p. 52 [reference to Louis Althusser, *Lénine et la philosophie, suivi de Marx et Lénine devant Hegel* (Paris: Maspero, 1972); cf. *Lenin and Philosophy and Other Essays*, trans. Ben Brewster (New York: Monthly Review Press, 1971), 64]."

perhaps the thetic character of the "Theses on Feuerbach" comes to be determined only in close relation to the content of what is uttered here, which would also therefore tell us what a *thesis* is, or rather what it must be, not what thesis (or *nomos*) means in opposition to *physis*, etc., etc., etc., or what an academic thesis is, or a position in Hegelian philosophy, but what a thesis, etc., must be. In short the 11th Thesis comes to be determined only within a context and the least that one can draw out of its immediate context is that the concept of practice and the theory/practice opposition plays a considerable and absolutely decisive role in it. The 1st Thesis reproaches an earlier materialism, that of Feuerbach in particular, for having grasped the object (*Gegenstand*), effectivity (*Wirklichkeit*) and sensuousness (*Sinnlichkeit*) only in the form of Object (*Objekt*) or intuition and not as praxis or sensuous human activity, that is to say "subjectively." One must not be misled by what is "subjective," it is here opposed to *Objekt*, not to *Gegenstand*, for further along grasping human activity as *praxis* means grasping it as objective activity (*gegenständliche Tätigkeit*). And this 1st Thesis also reproaches *The Essence of Christianity* for considering as "genuinely human [*echt menschlich*]" only the "theoretical attitude," or the theoretical relation or behavior (*das theoretische Verhalten*). The critique addresses Feuerbach but implicates everything in the history of philosophy that places the theoreticist [*théorétique*] attitude over and above the practical, seeing in the former the authentic or supreme human accomplishment, implicating, that is to say, perhaps the quasi-totality of philosophy, from Plato-Aristotle to Kant, including or excluding Kant, I'll leave that question open, we'll later see why. If this critique of theoreticism or theorizing implicates almost all of philosophy, another question remains open—and it is always open in a certain manner within the Marxist tradition—that of knowing whether this critique is still philosophical, belongs to something like philosophy, or abandons philosophy, suppresses or exceeds it. And the praxis in question, on the basis of which the critique of Feuerbach is stated, is itself determined only on the basis of an imperative, or if you prefer, the "revolutionary" rallying cry, in other words the determination of what is practical in praxis is not a theoretical determination but a determination that is itself practical and practico-revolutionary, determined by a "must," it must be done, where this doing—this will be the second emphasis that I'll come back to later—obtains its import from the "must" and not the other way round. What Feuerbach has failed to understand is the "meaning" (*Bedeutung*: sense and significance) of revolutionary activity, of "practical-critical" activity (*der praktisch-kritischen Tätigkeit*), where the critical instance itself (that is what the hyphen indicates) is itself conceived only "practically," in its practical, not its theoretical movement.

This theory/practice opposition is as it were the pivot of the ten theses that follow. For example, going very quickly for this first reading: 2nd Thesis: "The question whether objective truth can be attributed to human thinking is not a question of theory but is a *practical* (underlined) question. Man must prove the truth—i.e. the reality and power, the this-sidedness of his thinking [literally "on this side, here: *Diesseitigkeit seines Denkens*] in practice (*Praxis*). 3rd Thesis: "The coincidence [*Zusammenfallen*] of the changing [*ändern*: making other, becoming other, alteration—if that notion could avoid its connotation of degeneracy in French] of circumstances and of human activity or self-changing [*Selbstveränderung*] can be conceived and rationally understood only as *revolutionary practice* [revolutionäre Praxis]."[13]

That comes down to saying not only that all the predicates on whose basis one could try to circumscribe, in this context, what *praxis* means (namely, for instance, the predicates "activity," "subjective activity (by human subjects)," objective activity (*gegenständliche Tätigkeit*), values of truth, of thinking, etc., etc., predicates that seem to contribute to a definition of praxis by means of a network of traditional philosophemes), not only in fact are those predicates in turn, or should in turn be transformed, worked over, revolutionized by this revolutionary practice, this practically critical and revolutionary activity, <but also that> "revolutionary-practice"[14] constitutes an expression that is itself revolutionary in the sense that it would not be a matter of a practice whose meaning everybody already understood and that would come to obtain the precise sense of "revolutionary"—be unique by virtue of becoming revolutionary and receiving the predicate "revolutionary"—but rather a revolution-practice, that is a practice that would become practice, the practice that it must be, and provide access to its sense (theoretically) and to its being-practical of practice, only on the basis of revolutionary-practice. Revolutionary-practice alone can give access to practice, not so much to the essence of practice, to the meaning of practice, or even to the being-practical of practice, but rather to practice-practice, to a practice that can come to itself only from itself. In other words the sole practice on whose basis one can have access to practice (and having access no longer means here coming to think it theoretically, or to elucidate it semantically), the sole practice

---

13. Cf. Marx, "Theses on Feuerbach," 121.
14. [Translator's Note]: Here and below Derrida hyphenizes the two words to emphasize their conjointness.

that opens onto practice as such is revolutionary. One cannot even say—this would be a gross understatement—that one can think praxis only on the basis of revolution or revolutionary practice, for that would suppose that the final objective was to think correctly, to have a good theoretical concept of the meaning of practice (unless thinking isn't equivalent to theory, a question that we'll also come back to). No, one can practice practice only in a revolutionary way but revolution itself revolutionizes—in the context that concerns us at present—only by transforming practice in a revolutionary way, and starting from a transformed practice, from a new concept of practice, and, every concept being a theory/practice, from a new practice of practice.

When I speak here of context it is a question of a context or text that is not limited to the immediate context of the theses on Feuerbach, nor even of a text written on paper, but a non-closed set of differences in differ*a*nce, in the process of transformation, if you wish, and the value of alterity or difference in process, of differ*a*nce, is so central to this definition of practice that practice itself is defined on the basis of practice as revolutionary-practice and revolution as radical and total *Veränderung* (alteration) (of the world). If one calls text or open context in general (as I have done elsewhere) a network of relations to the other, of differ*a*nces and traces of differences, in a process of differ*a*nce, then the text or non-closed context is not here limited to what is understood by text in the everyday sense (what Marx, for example, wrote, as well as his notes, or drafts or complete works), but a field (the metaphor of a field no longer suffices since it usually serves to define regional contexts that are subject to a general science or philosophy), a text including everything that philosophy and the traditional language linked to it calls history, economy, politics, etc., etc. It is only starting from this non-closed text that "revolutionary-practice" in the "Theses on Feuerbach" will be able not only to be received, understood, decoded by some hermeneutic operation, but, and this is the sole reading that is appropriate here, to be practiced.

This enigmatic value of "practice"—enigmatic not because it would remain mysterious, inaccessible, deep, in-comprehensible,[15] but because it sets in motion a language that no longer simply requires being understood, received, conceived of, in the mode of a theoretical reading that is enigmatic because one doesn't know what it says and what it means before doing it, and even because one doesn't know *what* must be done, according to a rigorous anteriority, before doing it—this enigmatic value of "practice" is to

15. [Translator's note]: As such in typescript.

be found in almost all of the subsequent theses. I'll note very quickly its regularity, we'll no doubt come back to it later: concerning the secular basis (worldly: *weltliche Grundlage*) into which Feuerbach has "resolved" the religious world, and to explain that the secular basis is detached from itself in order to be established in the clouds as autonomous realm, that is in order to explain the phenomenon of religion, one must explain the cleavage and internal contradiction of this secular basis. But in order to understand that contradiction (understand and explain it: *verstehen, erklären*) one must *at once, both* (*sowohl . . . als* says Marx) understand it in its contradiction *and* revolutionize it practically: "*Diese* [secular basis] *selbst muß also in sich selbst sowohl in ihrem Widerspruch verstanden als praktisch revolutioniert werden.* Thus, for instance, after the earthly family is discovered as the secret of the holy family, *muß nun erstere selbst theoretisch und praktisch vernichtet werden*: the former must then itself be destroyed [reduced to nothing] theoretically and practically."[16] In other words, there is no theoretical critique without practical transformation (here without destruction). And no practice without transformation. As a result, in the last Thesis, the most famous, the most famous revolutionary "rallying cry," interpretation itself is what philosophers are said to be satisfied with (*nur . . . interpretiert*), an interpretation that will not even have been possible, as interpretation, without transformation, without transformative alteration. As a result one can also interpret this Thesis—practically—by saying, by translating, by transforming the utterance practically, going so far as to say: "Philosophers have not even succeeded in interpreting the world in various ways, what would be necessary [what will be necessary: the mood is difficult to establish, for essential reasons] to do [even to interpret it] is change it [*verändern*]."

The only question that I'll hold over—at least for the moment, following this scarcely even cursory reading of the "Theses"—the only question that interests me for today's discussion, is therefore the following one: does the last Thesis mark the end of philosophy (which would have been satisfied with interpreting) [comment], or the end of only the philosophy that is satisfied with interpreting, so that what Marx calls for would still be a philosophy,

---

16. Cf. Marx, "Theses on Feuerbach," 122: "But that the secular basis detaches itself from itself and establishes itself as an independent realm in the clouds can only be explained by the cleavages and self-contradictions within this secular basis. The latter must, therefore, in itself be both understood in its contradiction and revolutionized in practice. Thus, for instance, after the earthly family is discovered to be the secret of the holy family, the former must then itself be destroyed in theory and in practice." [Sentences preceding the quoted section, paraphrased by Derrida, have been added to provide context.]

but a philosophy that transforms the world, a practico-revolutionary philosophy. In short, in the first case, Marx would be calling for a general revolutionary practice and a revolutionary theory/practice that would no longer belong to the order of philosophy, essentially overflowing the philosophical as such; in the second, he would be calling for a practical revolutionary transformation of philosophy but without rejecting, suppressing, exceeding, destroying the philosophical. If that question has been guiding me for the time of this discussion it is because I would like to justify a first proposition, which consists in presenting Marxist discourse today, and dialectical materialism, as a *philosophy* (whatever its transformative or transformed novelty might be for putting into perspective the whole philosophical genealogy of the theory/practice pair), by interpreting-transforming history without abandoning the philosophical unity of the medium in which this history would need to be thought. I don't mean that this is the only way to read a Marxist text, much less the text of the "Theses on Feuerbach." But it is the way that I will call philosophical, that still gives the philosophical its due, and what I want to do, in the first place, is mark some reference points—two, as I said—for this potential reading. I don't know if what I am saying is already clear, but I hope that it will become so with the two examples or reference points that I announced.

The first is Gramsci's critique of Croce concerning the latter's proposed reading of the 11th Thesis. In his essay "Benedetto Croce and Dialectical Materialism" (1932–35) Gramsci cites Croce's *Critical Conversations*, where Croce analyzes the "Theses on Feuerbach" and concludes that in some way the subject of these theses, those who speak in them, "when confronted with preexisting philosophy, are not just more philosophers as one might expect, but practical revolutionaries." Croce goes on: "what Marx proposed was, precisely, to turn philosophy upside down—not just Hegel's philosophy [here Feuerbachian-Hegelian] but philosophy as a whole—and to replace philosophizing with practical activity."[17] Thus what Croce implies in this reading is that in Marx's eyes, in saying "the philosophers have only interpreted the world, etc.," Marx would intend: it is the essence of philosophy in general—and not simply the fact of philosophers, of some or all of them—to be satisfied with interpreting the world. Hence, if one must

---

17. [Translator's note]: Derrida cites Croce from Antonio Gramsci, "Benedetto Croce et le matérialisme historique," in *Gramsci dans le texte*, ed. F. Ricci (Paris: Éditions sociales, 1977), 402. See Antonio Gramsci, *Prison Notebooks*, vol. 3, ed. and trans. Joseph A. Buttigieg (New York: Columbia University Press, 1996), 348; cf. Antonio Gramsci, *Quaderni del carcere*, vol. 2 (Turin: Einaudi, 1975), 1270.

transform instead of interpret, that can be done only against or beyond philosophy in general. Conclusion: the "Theses" and dialectical materialism in general would no longer be essentially philosophical. That is what Gramsci protests against. I won't go into here—even though it would be necessary—the historical context of Gramsci's critique of Croce and the strategic necessity that guides one and the other on the basis of their respective positions. In light of the limited scope of my discussion today, I'll draw out how, for Gramsci, the 11th Thesis cannot be interpreted the way Croce interprets it, and that it is opposed, still philosophically (even if in a way that is absolutely new for philosophy), only to a theoretico-speculative philosophy, indeed to the theoretico-speculative tendency that dominates the history of philosophy. Gramsci writes:

> On the contrary [contrary to what Croce thinks about them], don't these theses make a claim, faced with "scholastic," purely theoretical or contemplative philosophy, for a philosophy that produces a morality in conformity with it, a will to realize with which it ultimately identifies. The 11th thesis ... cannot be interpreted as a repudiation of all philosophy, but simply as disgust for the parroting of philosophers [repetition/transformation] and as the vigorous affirmation of a unity between theory and practice. That such a solution coming from Croce is ineffective in critical terms can be demonstrated in this way: even if one admits by means of the absurd hypothesis, that Marx wanted to "replace" philosophy in general with practical activity, it would be necessary to "unsheathe" [*dégainer*: I suppose, not having the Italian, "undo," "extract oneself from"] the peremptory argument according to which one cannot deny philosophy except by philosophizing, that is to say by affirming what one wished to deny.[18]

The logic of the chiasmus at work here is that each position has its strengths and weaknesses. For a non- or anti-Marxist to say that Marxism suppresses philosophy may, in tribute to an apparent radicality, allow one to conclude that Marxism either remains in play for philosophy by becoming a pure and simple practical, indeed pragmatic, pre-theoretical or pre-critical empiricism (no more philosophy, just practical activity), or, which amounts to the same thing, that it remains philosophical in its disavowal, maintaining that philosophy had always trapped those who didn't want to be philosophers or who wanted to exceed philosophy: "one can deny philosophy only by

---

18. Gramsci, "Benedetto Croce et le matérialisme historique," 402; my translation. The Italian word translated here by *dégainer* is *sfoderare*, which Gramsci places within quotation marks. Cf. Gramsci, *Quaderni*, vol. 2, 1270.

philosophizing: *ei philopheteon, philosopheteon, kai ei mē philosopheteon, philosopheteon*."[19] Conversely, to affirm from revolutionary-Marxist positions that dialectical materialism is still a philosophy, and even the only possible one, the only one that includes-destroys the others practically, is to pay for theoretico-philosophical dignity by subscribing to the philosophical medium and to its own limits, including perhaps a congenital theoreticism. Whence the necessary effort for a general redistribution of theory/practice relations that avoids the effects of belonging to the traditional philosophical medium. I don't intend, nor am I able, to pursue this attempt by Gramsci today. I simply wanted to point out one of the places where dialectical materialism—inasmuch as it develops, practically, a theory/practice pair that it recognizes as playing a major organizing role in its discourse—interprets the history of philosophy practically and puts into perspective the history of this pair and of the dominance of theoreticism, putting it into perspective from a vantage [*bord*] that still wants to be philosophical.

The second reference point is more complex, I mean complex already as a reference point. For I don't mean to say, nor do I think that Gramsci's text is simple. Just that, for what interests us, his gesture was relatively simple.

We will have to look for the second reference point—next time—in a series of positions and in the systematic trajectory followed by Althusser. This reference cannot indeed be reduced to a point but is a trajectory. Such a trajectory is not something I'll claim to retrace, or even sum up here, I'll be satisfied with just taking from it, hoping not to betray its perspective, the elements that relate to our discussions this evening: 1. The relation to the event of the 11th Thesis; 2. The investment in concepts (or motifs) or in the theory/practice opposition as major concepts; 3. The question of what I was calling the philosophical edge [*bord*], of knowing whether or not, and in what way, dialectical materialism is a philosophy or philosophical practice (the critique addressed to Gramsci from this point of view and the redistribution of the problem). I'll refer essentially to "On the Materialist Dialectic" (in *For Marx*) (1965), to "Lenin and Philosophy" (1969) and the "Reply to John Lewis" (1973).[20] We'll try to draw some conclusions from

---

19. "If you should do philosophy, you should do philosophy; and if you should not do philosophy, then you should do philosophy." Attributed to Aristotle; cf. Aristotle, *Protrepticus or Exhortation to Philosophy*, ed. and trans. D. S. Hutchinson and Monte Ransome Johnson, 2017 (http://www.protrepticus.info/protr2017x20.pdf), 4.

20. Louis Althusser, "On the Materialist Dialectic," in *For Marx*, trans. Ben Brewster (London: Verso, 1970); "Lenin and Philosophy," in *Lenin and Philosophy and Other Essays*; "Reply to John Lewis," in *Essays in Self-Criticism*, trans. Grahame Lock (London: NLB, 1976). Further references to *For Marx*; *Lenin and Philosophy and Other Essays*;

that trajectory concerning what I was calling the genealogical-philosophical orientation of the theory/practice pair. Those conclusions will concern the structure of this philosophical edging [*bordure*]. We'll perhaps then see how this edging, its intricate structure—always exemplarily so concerning theory/practice—produces effects in the content that are different, but structurally analogous when viewed from another genealogical orientation, precisely in the text of a type that, going quickly, can be called Heideggerian ("The Question Concerning Technology," "Letter on 'Humanism,'" "Science and Meditation").[21]

We'll compare with that genealogical discussion, at least with its general type, not in order simply to oppose it, but to relate it to it according to another logic, another discussion, another orientation, another interpretation (at the same time theoretical and practical, if you wish, or neither one nor the other) of the theory/practice pair; again, it wouldn't simply be opposed to or separate from the other but something that exercises [*travaillerait*] it curiously and it is that work (if one can still call it work) that will interest us. In order to get closer to it, we would have to put a different emphasis on "must be done." So, it will have to be done, but in such a way that doing does not become accessible (theoretically, semantically, in its sense content, no more than practically) before or independently of the "must." "Must" is not a command or a prescription that would be attached to doing, to a doing whose meaning would be known. But if doing were to be preceded in advance—in its most essential content—by "must," there would perhaps follow from it certain consequences that we will examine. They will perhaps lead us to reread (but in the non-hermeneutico-theoretical sense that I give to that word), or if you prefer to rewrite otherwise—and especially not to neutralize them, but without subjugating them to philosophy, to the presumption of a unity of the philosophical medium—both the "Theses on Feuerbach" (and hence the whole Marxist text that opens) and problematics of the theory/practice pair such as those of psychoanalysis, speech acts or the performative, and consequently problematics that are in principle unlimited in number. Naturally, what I am there announcing ambitiously are risky paths, along which it will come to pass, I think, that I lose my way, and which, in any case, these few sessions can only sketch out in a summary and scarcely even preliminary way.

---

and *Essays in Self-Criticism* will be included in text. Translations are sometimes slightly modified to convey Derrida's emphasis.

21. [Translator's Note]: Parenthesis added by hand. See subsequent sessions of the seminar.

SECOND SESSION[1]

If I *say*: in theory some *blo*[2] (without any clarification, without any context), how will you hear it? How would you read it? What will you do with it? I don't know and I won't try to know. But it is a question.

I think more and more that the (practical and theoretical) *question* of context, and not only of the concept of context, will force us to deal with it throughout this seminar.

Next: a question, the *fact* or act of posing a question, of proposing an utterance in the form of a question, even a question whose object seems theoretical, is that a theoretical act? And is it a theoretical act that I engage in, or to which I invite you here by posing this question on the question? Is a problem, which isn't exactly a question, a theoretical problem, a problem whose content seems to be able to be determined as theoretical, is a problem theoretical? If a problem is the determination of an in-determination that lies before us, but before us not as a present object, as something that is already there, but as a *before* having [*comme* devant *devant*] to be determined, before having not yet to be completely before, prescribing, calling for the task of determination or resolution, legislating such a prescription, is a problem in itself theoretical or practical? There is a problem when I *am able to* determine the limits or edges of what I can't yet determine (in its content), but also when I *must* determine what I can't yet determine; when I can and must fore-see what I can't yet fore-see. If I fore-see everything there is no problem, no more than if I anticipate nothing. In the hypothesis

---

1. Derrida adds a handwritten and circled "TRA" at the top of the typescript. In the margin next to the first paragraph, he writes, "very slowly."

2. [Translator's Note]: *en théorie des cou*. Heard by itself the syntagma *cou* could refer in French to neck [*cou*], blow(s) [*coup(s)*], or throw as in throw of the dice [*coup de dés*]. Otherwise it is heard as the first syllable of many other words. In Derrida's typescript *coup* is written and struck out before *cou*.

of the theoretical as being always representable as being-before, as object for a gaze, is a problem—which is to say a before having not yet to be before, but having to become before [*devant devenir devant*]—theoretical or practical?

Theory looks. But there is a problem not only when it doesn't see everything it intends to look at, but also when somewhere, with no possible escape, the command is given to look, and when that command can no longer issue from the theory that looks, but from what looks at theory or *theōrein*, and *concerns* it.

This concerning [*concernement*], that is the command received to look where one neither yet sees or foresees, such a concerning has the decisive violence of the "it's my lookout [*ça me regarde*]" that removes from all theoretical legislation its practical status. When I say, when we say, when it is said "it's my lookout," "it's our lookout," "it concerns X or Y," there are said at least two things, among others, that can simultaneously or in turn sustain the emphasis of the utterance or its interpretation: incumbent practical responsibility (*ça me regarde* means it concerns me, the onus is on me, it's my affair, it's up to me to *do* it, it's my domain, that is to say the domain where it's up to me to act, to speak, to decide, etc., and even if that domain is a domain of theoretical activity, "it's my lookout" implies that I have practical responsibility for it); but simultaneously, and for the same reason I have authority over the domain for which I am responsible only to the extent that I am myself subject to a law and to something else, to the thing that is other, to the other-thing that looks at me, where I am (heteronomously) charged with a responsibility that I neither choose nor have control over. Moreover, in my being looked at from elsewhere [*le ça me regarde d'ailleurs*], my being looked at looking, we perhaps have there the practical instance that sets in motion the theoretical, even before it has, or even inasmuch as it has, and so that it has authority over its specific domain. *It's my lookout*, a "look-out of the theoretical gaze" perhaps precedes the theoretical gaze in order to constitute it from a practical standpoint. And saying, then, that our question, our problem would be: what is the *it* [*ça*] of *it looks*, it's my lookout, it's our lookout, it concerns looking, saying that we want to, or must know how things stand with this look, and about the *it* that concerns looking at the look, that is what locates us, or finds us already located in an exchange and in the space of a debt that most assuredly concerns the pair (theory/practice) but about which we would have difficulty deciding whether it is in and of itself theoretical or practical. In the final analysis is the determination of the "it" theoretical or practical? What is in any case certain is that such a determination renders impossible any settled or conciliatory symmetry between theory and practice.

And if the practical order of "it's my lookout" or "must be done" precedes every theoretical movement, and even every theoretical contemplation, being encompassed by and implicated in it in advance, that means that the theoretical begins, if not by being blinded then at least by seeing only on the basis of the thing—the other-thing—that concerns it. Where the theoretical, therefore, no longer fore-sees or else fore-sees only by being foreseen by what it doesn't fore-see.

Whence the necessity, fatality, chance or fortune (they can no longer be distinguished here), whence the dice-throw by which a theoretical initiative always, somewhere, begins. Whence the dice-throw that must govern the economy of theory/practice relations once looking, lucidity, foresight, theoretical anticipation is necessarily blind in some respect, blind not so much with respect to something that it doesn't see, but with respect to a place, that of another gaze that precedes it, and that is not at theory's disposal. That structural unforeseeability, which situates the theoretical gaze and limits it as if from the inside, is the space and necessity of the throw of dice. And the theory of blo(ws) [*cou(ps)*] itself can found its economy only on a throw of the dice.

I don't therefore claim, especially not, to justify, precisely [*justement*]— and I say that so as not to justify it—my taking as a starting point for a seminar on Theory and Practice something that might have been judged random or arbitrary, the popular French expression *faut le faire*.

Faut le faire/ça me regarde: that is the subject.

I won't go back over what was proposed last week. Simply this, that we were in the process of exploring, proceeding toward a first phase of emphasis of *must be done* that caused the accent to be placed on *doing*: what is needed? Doing. We were exploring one of two problematic possibilities, the one I called the semantico-philosophical genealogy. Within that *philosophical* problematic I tried to justify my point of departure in a Marxist conceptuality, within the current form of dialectical materialism. I proposed two points of reference having this in common: a shared reference to those enigmatic textual utterances or events entitled "Theses on Feuerbach," and we wondered how they would have to be interpreted or transformed. The first reference point was Gramsci's critique of Croce's interpretation and the former's affirming (I mean his practical affirmation, as political optative, as political and philosophical position) a Marxist philosophy of praxis. The second reference point I announced, that I was getting to, was Althusser's unmarked [*non ponctuel*] trajectory. I explained why I said "trajectory" and that we would analyze in particular what in it seemed pertinent to our problematic: 1. the relation to the event of the 11th Thesis; 2. the investment in the theory/practice pair as a major or last recourse philosophical motif; 3. the question of the philosophical edge and knowing whether or not, and in what respect, materialism is a philosophy or philosophical practice.

Althusser's text entitled "On the Materialist Dialectic" (1963, republished in *Pour Marx* in the "Théorie" Collection) has as its epigraph the following quote from the 8th Thesis on Feuerbach[3]: "All mysteries which lead theory to mysticism find their rational solution in human practice and in the comprehension of this practice."[4] The German is: *Alle Mysterien* [All mysteries], *welche die Theorie zum Mystizismus veranlassen* [that is: which lead theory to mysticism: *veranlassen* was changed by Engels to *verleiten*,[5] an interesting correction but it wasn't kept by the publishers or by those who later quoted Marx in the original version of his text, then, even though the title "Theses," inspired by Engels, has come, conversely, to be imposed on the text; *verleiten*, then, a word chosen by Engels, means to mislead, to lead (*conduire*) off the path, one could almost say se-duce, induce away from the normal and correct path, lead up a garden path (*dé-voyer*), mysticism here being considered by Engels as a depravation of theory, which must then be put back on the right path], I'll continue, then: "All mysteries which lead theory to mysticism *finden ihre rationelle Lösung,* [find their rational solution or resolution] *in der menschlichen Praxis* [in human practice] *und im Begreifen dieser Praxis.*"[6] This Thesis, then, seemingly very *practicist*, nevertheless contains this practicism within very rigorous limits, and I suppose that Althusser wanted to draw attention as much to the practicism as to its limits and conditions when he placed this Thesis as the epigraph to a text that, at the time and in that specific situation, must have functioned as a call to theoretical rigor and to the practical imperative of that theoretical rigor for Marxist discourse and Marxist practice. On the basis of what can one recognize these very rigorous limits and conditions imposed on the practicism of the 8th Thesis? On the basis of at least two signs. First sign (on the blackboard). It is a matter of determining where things stand with

---

3. [Translator's Note]: The margin contains the following handwritten additions: "Alt<husser>, blackboard," and further down barely legible words, perhaps "mysticism and ideology."

4. Louis Althusser, *Pour Marx* (Paris: François Maspero, 1965); cf. *For Marx*, 161; Marx, "Theses on Feuerbach," 122.

5. Friedrich Engels, "Karl Marx über Feuerbach," in *Ludwig Feuerbach und der Ausgang der klassischen deutschen Philosophie* (Stuttgart: Dietz, 1888), 72. See also Marx, "Thesen über Feuerbach," in *Marx-Engels Gesamtausgabe*, vol. 3 (Berlin: Dietz, 1978), 535.

6. Marx, "Thesen über Feuerbach," 535.

practice and with the necessity of practice. The short sentence, the first of the Thesis, that precedes the extract cited by Althusser says, "All social life is essentially *practical* [Marx's emphasis]."⁷ Now, this practical instance is not here in opposition to theory, far from it, but to what leads theory to mysticism. Human practice is not opposed to theory but to a possible effect of theory, the effect called mysticism. Marx can consider that effect as possible or inevitable, as inscribed or not in the autonomous development of theory, but he doesn't qualify it further. For his part, Engels wades right in, and by substituting *verleiten* for *veranlassen* he makes clear that he considers that effect to be a perversion, leading astray, a pathology on the part of theory. To counter that pathology or mystical perversion that lies in wait for all theory one must have recourse to human practice. Thus, theory is not mystical in and of itself. And if mystique or mystical contemplation is opposed to rationality, theory in itself is rational and must return to being rational, cured by practice of its perversion or in any case of its mystical effects. Practice is therefore in the service of rationality, it is in itself rational, as much as is theory. In order to get back to rationality, the rational solution, says Marx, in order to get back to a theoretical rationality perverted by or in mystique, to straighten it out, human practice is necessary. Mysticism is the wrong [*tort*], the torsion, turning away theoretical rationality, practice is the right made straight or the wrong made straight of that rationality, which theory should have maintained, and which it can and must get back to. There you have the first sign of this rigorous limitation of practicism. It must be rational and rationality manifests itself as much in the form of (rigorous, not perverted) theory as in the form of practice. Rationality is practical and theoretical; it is a value that is in a way anterior and superior—to the extent that it is invoked here—to the value both of the theoretical and the practical. It is a final recourse. *In itself* it is no more theoretical than practical. Naturally, that statement has to be understood in context, within its contextual system. The same utterance could be found elsewhere and mean something totally different, or *in any case seem to mean something completely different*. The substance of it can be found in Kant or in Husserl. When Kant divides philosophy into theoretical and practical rationality he indeed implies that reason in itself, to the extent that it is equivalent to philosophy, reason in itself exists anterior to the theory/practice opposition. But then, how the fundamental anteriority of reason is subsequently distributed in an always dissymmetrical way within what it founds and what determines

---

7. Marx, "Theses on Feuerbach," 122.

it (theoretical or practical reason) is something we'll have to ask ourselves later in reading Kant closely, and in particular by reading at least three texts.

1. The preface to the *Foundations of the Metaphysics of Morals* and the whole demonstration there that upholds the thesis that theoretical reason (or speculative reason) and practical reason have a common principle and in fact form one and the same reason: "I require that the critique of a pure practical reason . . . be able to present its unity with speculative reason in a common principle; because in the end there can be only one and the same reason, which must differ merely in its application."[8] It remains that—as in Marx, although the sense of "as" may seem completely different—this unity of reason (Reason in general, cf. beginning of Transcendental Dialectic: Can we isolate reason? *Kann man die Vernunft isolieren?*)[9] that is the final common recourse (since in the 8th Thesis the practical rational solution must be found for a theoretical process that leads, naturally or perversely, to mysticism), this unity of a reason that is not then in itself more theoretical than practical will be found, in Kant, as in Marx, better represented, more satisfied by practical than by theoretical reason. Even if it doesn't function the same way in each of the two discourses, the hierarchy that subordinates the theoretical to the practical imposes on each an analogous formal structure, and that formality will have to be questioned; it will be necessary to see how this practicism is rigorously de-limited and given rigorous theoretical limits.

2. One of the other places to analyze in the Kantian corpus from this point of view will be, for example, the end of *<The Critique of> Pure Reason*, in the "Transcendental Doctrine of Method," chapter II, section II: "On the ideal of the highest good, as a determining ground of the ultimate end of pure reason." As you know, Kant wonders there whether reason couldn't, in its practical interest, give us what it refuses in its speculative interest. And it is then that he speaks of the interest of reason, and this value of interest is, I should say, interesting in the extreme, to the extent that it names an *interest* that is as yet determined neither as theoretical nor as practical, but which, as interest, seems to have more affinity or analogy with a practical finality than with a theoretical finality. You know—and I'm only recalling this to situate problems that we will, I hope, work on further—that Kant defines these

---

8. Immanuel Kant, *Groundwork of the Metaphysics of Morals*, trans. and ed. Mary Gregor and Jens Timmermann (Cambridge: Cambridge University Press, 2012), 7.

9. [Translator's Note]: This parenthesis is a handwritten marginal insertion. Cf. Immanuel Kant, *Critique of Pure Reason*, trans. and ed. Paul Guyer and Allen W. Wood (Cambridge: Cambridge University Press, 1998), 390.

interests of my reason in the form of questions. One must be attentive to the fact that the utterance here defining something, namely interests, the interests of reason, of *my* reason, has an interrogative form, which is a strange way to define a content; and further, that the interest so defined by present tense interrogative utterances (What can I know? What should I do? What may I hope?) relate to the first person, they are questions posed by an *I*, now, defining *my* reason in the form of a question, not reason in general but *my* reason, and *my reason* in general, the interests of *my-reason* in general. "*Alles Interesse meiner Vernunft* [all interest of my reason, says Kant, and, within parentheses: the speculative as much as the practical] comes together, is united (*vereinigt sich*) in the following three questions:

1. *Was kann ich wissen?*
2. *Was soll ich tun?*
3. *Was darf ich hoffen?* what am I permitted to hope."[10]

The first question is speculative, the second, which also belongs to pure reason, is practical, but the third, in this sense closer to the interest in general of my reason in general, is, Kant says, at once practical and theoretical (*praktisch und theoretisch zugleich*). Hope then, or rather being-able-to-hope, the right to hope, has or is alleged to have an essential relation to the unity of reason inasmuch as the latter is both practical and theoretical. And here one must think not only hope but "I am permitted to hope" as an interest of reason that is at the same time theoretical and practical. And since we already know that not only the question of the mode of enunciation but also the no less enigmatic question of the event should be a focus of this seminar, let us see very quickly how Kant defines hope. Hope, he says, tends toward happiness and it has the same relation to the practical order and to moral law as do knowing and natural law to the theoretical knowledge of things. And the practical order, the practical, leads like a "main thread [*Leitfaden*]" to the solution of the theoretical, to the response (*Beantwortung*) of the theoretical and, once this question of the theoretical arises, to the speculative question.[11] This is in a way an analogous structure to that of the 8th Thesis, where the practical, the recourse to "human practice," serves as rational solution (*rationelle Lösung*) to the mysteries issuing from theory. I indeed said "an analogous structure." The analogy of practical mediation leading

---

10. Cf. Kant, *Pure Reason*, 677: "What can I know? What should I do? What may I hope?"
11. Cf. Kant, *Pure Reason*, 677.

to the theoretical solution or response is clear. But if practice and theory were to mean something different in Kant and in Marx, the analogy would be purely formal. We indeed sense that "practice" doesn't cover the same semantic field in Kant as in Marx. But, on the one hand, it is not yet clear that they don't share some common essential core (the value of interest, hope, and relation to the other of the *Veränderung*, of transformation, give us at least some indications that will have to be looked at more closely); and, on the other hand, a purely formal analogy that at least involves common vocabulary and logical syntax cannot be absolutely insignificant, absolutely unconnected to content. See, still provisionally, how Kant defines hope in this passage. He defines it rather curiously as what causes something to be, what ends up (*hinausläuft*) with the fact that something *is* (in the present of being, of the verb to be), for something has to *come about* [arriver], *weil etwas geschehen soll*. Definition of hope by means of arrival, of the event, the history of what comes (*geschehen, Geschichte*), but also what must arrive, necessity of a future constituted by what comes, what arrives. In starting out from this to-come [*à-venir*] of coming the *is*, the present of the *is* gets defined in this strange structure of hope. The event to-come there precedes, as it were, the determination of the present, a determination that is itself necessarily given here in the theoretical mode of *is*; whereas, different from hope, knowledge ends up (*hinausläuft*) with the conclusion that something is (acts as ultimate cause) because something comes about (*weil etwas geschieht*). In the present. In knowledge the present of the event determines the present, and "because [*weil*]" functions there quite differently. The fact that, in the case of *hope*, "because" has a rational function (purely rational and both theoretical and practical), a rational function that calls for a future "come" of the event, for a to-come of the event, for a history (*Geschichte*) of the *Geschehen* to come, and that opens thus from this to-come onto the unity between reason and the interest of my-reason in general, that fact means that "because" (*weil* rather) is invested with a very strange function and significance. One is then less surprised—I refer you to it with this brief mention—to discover (especially in *Der Satz vom Grund*, translated as *The Principle of Reason*) Heidegger's insistent detour, which might seem baroque or adventurous, through a meditation on the word *weil* in German, a word in which he sees appear the essence of reason and of the abyss of reason.[12] He does that, as you know, by meditating on "without"

---

12. Martin Heidegger, *Der Satz vom Grund* (Pfullingen, Germany: Verlag Gunther Neske, 1957), 77–79; cf. *The Principle of Reason*, trans. Reginald Lilly (Bloomington: Indiana University Press, 1996), 41–42.

in Angelus Silesius's supposed mystical formula: *Die Ros ist ohn warum; sie blühet, weil sie blühet / Sie acht nicht ihrer selbst, fragt nicht, ob man sie siehet*: The rose is without why but it isn't without reason, and it is by putting a different emphasis on the two "withouts" of the *sine ratione*, of "nothing is without reason" (Leibniz) of the principle of reason, that Heidegger causes the abyss to appear, the *Abgrund* of the *Grund*, the abyss of a reason that is reason only by not having reason (ground [*fond*] without ground). His rereading of "because" works through what he calls the proper sense of *weil*, which properly speaking (*eigentlich heist*) means *dieweilen* (while, whereas), as in the expression *Man muß das Eisen schmieden, weil es warm ist* (strike while the iron is hot, and not because it is hot). *Weilen* properly means to last, stay still, endure, stop, hold there, as in the line from Goethe quoted by Heidegger: *Die Fiedel stockt, der Tänzer weilt*, the violin falls silent, the dancer stops (hesitates, suspends his movement and stops). On that basis Heidegger draws attention to the fact that *weilen* (remain, last, endure: *währen, immerwähren*) is the old sense of the verb "to be" in German, with the result that—I'm abridging a great deal but it's just in order to provide some problematic directions—*weil* names being as ground, then as ground without ground, being that obtains a ground only by itself being without ground, without reason, etc. If we come back to Kant here, and to the elucidation of this reason in general that is at the same time theoretical and practical, therefore in itself pre-theoretico-practical, this reason whose theoretico-practical unity is better demonstrated through this form of interest called hope (and you can well see that *hope*, as a privileged form of my-reason in general [theoretico-practical] in its fundamental interest, that hope here no longer designates some vague pathos, affect, or sentimentality), if then we come back to Kant and to the elucidation of this reason in its pre-theoretico-practical originarity such as is demonstrated in hope, or rather in the question "what am I permitted to hope," then *weil*, what is translated by *by* (by reason of that which [*par ce que*]) indeed reinforces the trajectory, the course, the place. It is in the *by* [par], I would say, concerning the track-switching of *by*, through the switching function of *by* in by reason of, in *weil*, that it gets divided, I mean that we are going to be able to make a distinction between the relation of hope to the event and the relation of knowledge to the event. I'll again read two sentences from Kant:

> For all *hope* concerns happiness, and with respect to the practical and the moral law it is the very same as what knowledge and the natural law is with regard to theoretical cognition of things. The former finally comes down to the inference [*Schluß*: logical conclusion], that something *is* [soit:

sei: grammatical commentary] (which determines the ultimate final end) *because* (weil) *something ought to happen* [etwas geschehen soll]; the latter (knowledge) comes down to this conclusion, that something *is* [sei] (which acts as the supreme cause [*oberste Ursache*]) *because* [weil] *something does happen*.[13]

So in both cases, hoping and knowing, the conclusion that something *is* depends on a relation to the event, to "something comes to pass": in one case something *ought to* come to pass; in the other something comes to pass (effectively, presently). But in both cases the form of the relation of conclusion to event (present or future), the form of the *necessary* relation to the two necessary events—one being necessary as *geschehen sollen*, the other as ultimate cause—the form of the relation of conclusion to event is that of a *weil* (by/by reason of/because). In both cases something is, it is concluded that something is or might be [*soit*] (*sei*) *because* (weil) something ought to come to pass or something does come to pass. *Weil* is therefore the immobile place, or rather than an immobile place, an immobile apparatus for a trajectory that divides, what I called just now a switching function, a fixed but articulated syntagma that sometimes relates to the future of the event, sometimes to the present of the event, and which is therefore reason, the relation of reason to what comes, to what comes to pass in general, whether in the present or the future. Not only the relation of *reason*, rather the relation of *my*-reason, the interest of my-reason in what comes, and which, as a result, is no longer a neutral coming in the sense of an absolutely impersonal coming, but what, coming to my-reason, is also interpellated by me, by a non-empirical me, the I of my-reason that must somewhere say "come" to what comes in this way, providing the place here for knowledge, there for hope.

Naturally this switching through *by* (its double unity), through which the theoretical and/or practical interest of my-reason transits, is much less perceptible—or its switching unity is much less perceptible—in the French translation, where *weil* is translated in one case by *puisque* and in the other by *parce que*.

By is one of those little words through which, by which will pass most of the axes of our problematic. What can it mean to say that it passes by *by*? Not that the solution to the problems will be verbal or philological, nor that it will suffice to question a word, a preposition, even yet a verb or noun,

---

13. Kant, *Pure Reason*, 677.

a preposition, that it will be sufficient to analyze it to find the "rational solution." No, but it will in any case be necessary to know what does or does not pass by *by*, what does or does not come to pass in the distribution of these *bys*. You perhaps remember—well, those who were here last year remember—everything that intersected in the line from Ponge:

> By the word *by* begins then this text [*Par le mot* par *commence donc ce texte*]
> Whose first line tells the truth,
> But this tain beneath the one and the other
> Can it be tolerated?
> Dear reader already you judge
> There our difficulties . . .
>
> (AFTER *seven years of misfortunes*
> *She shattered her mirror*.)[14]

I am not going to return to the analysis of that "Fable" (title of the fable) but will simply note in that regard that the impossibility of producing a metalanguage concerning *by*, the impossibility of speaking of *by* without already passing by it, using the word one wants to speak of, that structural impossibility has an essential relation—which could be demonstrated if we had time—to the shattering of the mirror, both to the effect of the mirror, an effect that is specular or speculative (theoretical if you wish), and to its shattering interruption which can come about only with a single blow, in an event, an event that repeats and translates the initial event: by the word by that constitutes a false speculum, a false speculation that doesn't succeed in seizing its object and, for that very reason, forms the event of a text, an event-text that no theoretical metalanguage can surprise except by allowing itself to be occupied in advance, preoccupied *by* it, by *by*. No theoretical metalanguage but no *metapractice*. Etc.

If one can foresee that *by* will be a heavy traffic zone for our analyses it is at least for the reason that if the *par* of *parce que*, which signifies the interest of reason, an interest that always proceeds *by*, if this *by* translates *weil* only imperfectly (perhaps losing something of its distant reference to duration), it indeed retains in any case the significance of what persists [*perdure*] or tends to permanence [*per*mane] through a change or alteration or

---

14. Francis Ponge, "Fable," in *Le parti pris des choses, suivi de Proêmes* (Paris: Gallimard, 2006), 126; my translation.

movement; it indeed retains its *per*. Retaining the *per* here means keeping the sense of traversing, crossing, of what is accomplished by, that is to say through [*à travers*]. The value of *trans*, of *tra*, which is intimately commingled with that of *per*, and in which are found at least the senses of movement as pathway through, as crossing, as achieving by acquitting oneself, getting to the end, accomplishing, *per*forming, *per*fecting, finishing, succeeding, ending up (look at Kant's text: hope and knowledge end with the conclusion, *läuft hinaus by*, because, etc.), all those values of by, *per*, *trans*, *tra* that we will come across again in all the semantic motifs that are indissociably connected by modernity to *practice*, namely, especially, the values of trans-formation or, through complicated lexicological relays to that of labor [*travail*], tripalium (torture) → passivity, suffering [comment],[15] in which each time one rediscovers the idea of passing by and therefore also passing beyond, *trans* implying crossing [*traversée*], laborious, difficult, painful travel[16] or travail, and passing beyond. *Per* and *tra*—the process (comment on these two senses . . .[17] step and law of the thing) by which one might think modernity weighs down the concept of praxis—are to be found in the semantic functioning of *praxis* in Greek. If one looks, in a totally preliminary way, at the different acceptations of the verb *prassō*, even before deriving from it *praxis*, which, as we shall see, Plato and Aristotle would oppose sometimes to *pathos*, other times to *logos*, or to *theōria*, or *poiēsis*, or *proairesis* (project), following more subtle and problematic inflections than is usually noted, if then before even analyzing *praxis* one makes a simple preliminary and superficial list of the acceptations of *prassō*, one can draw out the whole semantic spectrum of what is called, or has been called "practice" throughout Western history. That whole spectrum is deployed by *by*, through the seme of crossing or passage through and beyond. If I say it is deployed by *by* or through *through*, through traversing [*à travers la traversée*] it is not to make a game of it, but because the sense is in fact transformed by passing through the schema of transformation and *trans*, as one would say in Latin, at once passage through and overflow, transgression, the step that surpasses [*pas de dépassement*]. Here is the list of those transformations (I am not citing the examples found in the dictionary but just the semantic rubrics): *prassō*: 1. to go through, pass through, cross, travel down a path, make a trip; 2. consequently: go to the very end, complete, execute, accomplish, do, in opposition

---

15. [Translator's Note]: Lat. *tripalium* is the etymological source for such words as the French *travail*.

16. [Translator's Note]: In English in the original.

17. [Translator's Note]: Ellipsis in typescript.

to *legō*.¹⁸ The examples of accomplishing, doing, executing are just as valid for murder, a good deed, or obscenity; there is even an interesting tautology (in Aeschines of Athens, for example):¹⁹ *tēn praxin prassein* or *prattein* is— I'm here quoting, must be done, the dictionary—to do the thing, in other words make love, practice the practice, meaning to do the thing, and, in the order of desire, which is perhaps the essential order of practice, move on to the act [*passer à l'acte*], the sexual act being perhaps not just one act among others, one practice among others, no more than would the passage to the act be a divisible expression, if the passage is, as crossing through, always a passage as act, a passing on to the act, and if the act always implies, as practice, a crossing, then every act is a passage, as crossing and as transgression.

If, to the extent that it engages and involves a body that doesn't reduce to Hegel's theoretical senses—sight and hearing, opposed to the senses he calls practical (touch, smell and taste)²⁰—if sexual practice is not one example of practice among others, then you'll get the sense here that the question of work and of the division of labor, and of the sexual division of labor within the Marxist problematic, a set of questions that we looked into together here two years ago,²¹ this set of questions that we will find again is indeed a systematic set and not localizable as particular or derivative. We already perceive, by anticipation, what the second emphasis will be, the second inflection of *must be done*. It insists on transgression: when one says *faut le faire* one can also imply, it's implied half the time: you've got some nerve [*faut être gonflé*], he's got some set [il *est gonflé-le-mec*],²² or, less commonly, she's got some set, which still often implies—within the phallocentric space that often determines the value of transgression, of cheek [*culot*]—that chick is a real stud [*mec*]; *faut le faire* is what one exclaims when confronted with cheek, transgressive boldness, he or she dared *do* that, he or she didn't get cold feet. We'll come back to that. I'll now return to the list of acceptations: it moves on to *act, work, busy oneself with*, act in the interest of, take care of one's business (public or private); then: accomplish, complete, realize, carry through (hence see through to the end), then (here there is an important inflection, it seems to me, for our subsequent work), to cause, acquit, have (a debt, tax, interest) paid, demand, require to be paid, hence

---

18. Derrida's source is Anatole Bailly, *Abrégé de dictionnaire grec-français* (Paris: Hachette, 1950).

19. [Translator's Note]: Closing parenthesis added by editor.

20. A marginal handwritten addition here appears to read: "Get one's hands dirty [*y mettre la main*], and one's feet, step out walking, step/not [*pas*]."

21. Derrida appears to refer to his 1973–74 seminar on "Art (Kant)."

22. [Translator's Note]: Hyphenated in Derrida's typescript.

cause to be punished (expiate for a crime, pay for, etc.), but this sense can also be taken, as the dictionary says, in a negative sense and function for "to finish off [*achever*], cause to perish."

Perishing or causing to perish is moreover interesting to the extent that it links the idea of death and murder to that of the passage beyond, of a transgressive process, of what passes beyond, to the idea of practice as passing away [*trépas*], etc.

I'll finish here this opening concerning *weil* and *by*. I hope at least to have convinced you that it was an inescapable opening onto the problem of practice, of theory/practice, of the interest of reason that is at stake in Kant's text, and onto the rational solution that, according to the 8th Thesis quoted by Althusser as an epigraph, human practice brings to theory when the latter leads to mysticism.

But we haven't finished with Kant, not even today's obligatory little detour. You will have in any case understood, I hope, why last week I left hanging the question of knowing whether with Kant (whether it was excluded or included, I said) the presumed continuum of the history of philosophy did or did not recognize a rupture on whose basis the Marxist value of *practice* was or was not going to be transformed and be decisively extracted from its traditional semantic milieu. In any case the passage through Kant is essential. Even if, which goes without saying or is at least very clear, practice does not mean the same thing in Marx and in Kant, far from it; clarification of the practical instance, of the "pure(ly) practical" in Kant cannot not have an essential relation to the historical and philosophical space within which the 8th Thesis on Feuerbach, and the rest of dialectical materialism, occur.

As I was saying, we haven't even finished with today's little preliminary detour through Kant. I still wanted to situate (that's all I can do for the moment) two texts by Kant, two other texts by Kant.[23]

In Book II of the Transcendental Dialectic, chapter II, 3rd section, entitled "Of the Interest of Reason in These Conflicts," one finds a certain passage, a certain form of argumentation that perhaps has some significance in relation to the 8th Thesis on Feuerbach, that can be brought to bear on it both from the point of view of the concept, of conceptual discourse, and from the point of view of rhetoric, even of *metaphoric*. In that chapter, then, it is still a matter of the interest of reason, but from the point of view of the

---

23. [Translator's Note]: Derrida begins the following paragraph with the number 1, but the second text referred to here is in fact the introduction to the *Critique of Judgment*, discussion of which begins on p. 35 below as number 3, according to the numbering begun above on p. 24.

conflicts that put it in opposition with itself. I'll presume that the transcendental dialectic is already known. We have here a fundamental explanation of the origin of this conflict. That conflict is unfortunate, says Kant, unfortunate at least for speculation, even if for the practical vocation of man it is favorable. I can't go back over the whole complex trajectory of the chapter, which considers in turn dogmatism on the side of the thesis and empiricism on the side of the antithesis, and considers them in turn from the point of view of practical interest and of speculative interest, then the opposition between Epicurianism and Platonism. I'll pick it up in the final two paragraphs, where Kant affirms that human reason is, by nature, architectonic; which means that its preoccupation with the system is major. Reason considers that all knowledge belongs to a possible system. But the propositions of the antithesis, in each antinomy, have the effect of rendering architectonics, that is to say systematicity, *impossible*; it is antithesis that proposes that over and above the state of the world there is a more originary, still older one, in each part, and that the parts are in turn divisible, another event before each one, etc., without ever encountering any unconditioned (*unbedingtes*) or absolute beginning that could serve as foundation for the systematic edifice. That is why the thesis—in contrast to the antithesis—is more in conformity with the architectonic interest of reason. There is then a natural tendency in the interest of reason for the thesis, for the moment of the antinomy that is called the thesis.[24] Let's now imagine a reason without interest; a reason that would have emancipated itself from all interest. It is on the basis of that hypothesis that we can imagine what interest is (thinking its outline on the basis of the hole it leaves), and it is especially by starting from there that we are going to see the privileged link between the notion or value of the interest-of-reason (pure, in general) and practical, rather than speculative reason. So Kant asks: what would a man do if he could emancipate himself from every interest and remain indifferent to all the consequences of theses and antitheses, if the interest of reason in him were therefore suspended, up to and including architectonic interest, interest in the system. Such a man would follow only the principles of reason wherever they led him, taking into account their intrinsic value alone, their value as rational principle. What would happen in such a case? Well, such a man would have to follow alternately the thesis and the antithesis. He would be caught in the double bind of a reason without interest. He would be, Kant says, in a state of ceaseless vacillation: *in einem unaufhörlich schwankenden*

---

24. Cf. Kant, *Pure Reason*, 502.

Zustand.²⁵ The double bind, which is the double tie, the double obligation to follow contradictory rational principles, that double bind would here be rational and based on principle; a double bind of pure reason. And yet, when Kant says "ceaseless vacillation" between two principles of equal value he also means—the two principles being exactly concurrent—that such a man, such a disinterested reason would simultaneously be stretched to the breaking point between the principles of two demands and two consequences. Today this, tomorrow that, says Kant, but it is in order to provide a temporal image of a synchronous, simultaneous tension, causing one to be convinced, for example, that human freedom is free *and* that in the indissoluble chain of nature freedom is but an illusion, that there is only nature. Such a disinterested reason thinks those two things alternately or simultaneously. How to escape from this theoretico-speculative double bind? Well, replies Kant, by means of practice. This double bind is in fact a speculative game, a game of speculative reason and this game produces—here is the formulation that I wanted to bring to bear on the 8th Thesis on Feuerbach—"the phantoms of a dream [*die Schattenbilder eines Traumes*],"²⁶ that is to say a sort of visionary effect, a sort of mystical hallucination. And the solution, resolution/dissolution of this mystical effect of speculative reason is practice. Practice is the rational solution to the visionary effects of theoretical speculation, of pure speculative reason. Having evoked the ceaseless vacillation between thesis and antithesis, the dizziness of alternating between one and the other that would plague a disinterested rational man, Kant then writes: "But if he [such a man] were to come to practice [translation for *zum Tun und Handeln*: act and do, deal with, manipulate, move on to action], this game of a purely speculative reason would vanish like the phantoms of a dream [like the shadows, figures or silhouettes of a dream], and he would choose his principles merely according to practical interest." Following that, Kant specifies that that is not a reason to immediately renounce the exercise of pure speculative reason, neither the exercise nor the time dedicated to this examination of pure speculative reason, to its theses and antitheses such as behooves a reflective being, one concerned with research. Besides, it is good to develop theses and antitheses freely, free of threat, and to defend them in

---

25. Cf. Kant, *Pure Reason*, 503: "But if a human being could renounce all interests, and, indifferent to all consequences, consider the assertions of reason merely according to their grounds, then, supposing that he knows no way of escaping the dilemma except by confessing allegiance to one or the other of the conflicting doctrines, such a person would be in a state of ceaseless vacillation."

26. Kant, *Pure Reason*, 503.

the presence of a jury of one's peers, that is to say fallible men (democracy, etc. . . .).²⁷ No more than did Marx, Kant doesn't want here to disqualify the speculative at the moment when he is saying that practice causes its mystical or visionary clouds—dreaming—to disperse. Whatever the difference in conceptual content between the Kantian concept of practice and that of Marx in the "Theses on Feuerbach," a difference that we will have to specify, it remains that the analogy in the organization of their argumentation is not just formal in the sense of an exterior overlay. It also affects the content, and implies necessarily a system of common traits within the concepts of practice, interest, theory, in the relation between theory and practice, in the visionary effect of contradiction in theory, etc. What does that analogy refer us to, that is the question that I wanted to pose by bringing into the discussion and situating in this way a second text by Kant.

3. The third place to reconnoiter, to situate in Kant's writing, is the Preface and Introduction to the *Critique of Judgment* that had, among other functions, that of insuring by means of teleology, by the concept of finality, something like the transition or mediation between purely theoretical and purely practical reason. A detailed reading of the *Critique of Judgment* and first of all of its preface and introduction concerning the Division of Philosophy (into theory and practice) is, would be, will be indispensable for what interests us in this seminar. In concluding today I will simply point to the specificity of the concept of *technē* (art or technique) that comes to rigorously divide that of practice, thereby making it more precise and identifying one of the essential loci of our problem, the question of technique, of the place of technique between theory and practice. Just two indications to situate the transitions [*aiguillages*] in the *Critique of Judgment*: 1. The Introduction on the Division of Philosophy, into theoretical philosophy or philosophy of nature and practical or moral philosophy founded on the concept of freedom; and within that introduction the need to distinguish within practical principles those that are practical *technically* (concept of natural causality) and those that are practical morally (concept of freedom). This division in the concept of practice between its moral and technical values is clearly an important split for this whole problematic; 2. Second place, §43 ("On art in general"), the distinction between art and nature that deploys

---

27. Cf. Kant, *Pure Reason*. [Translator's note]: Ellipsis in typescript. For the quoted sentence, the English translation has the following: "But now if it came to be a matter of doing or acting, then this play of purely speculative reason would disappear like the phantom images of a dream, and he would choose his principles merely according to practical interest."

all the concepts that are, in general, vaguely confused, precisely by means of a confusion regarding the concept of practice (doing, operating, acting, producing, etc.) including all the possible combinations from one language to another. Restricting himself to Latin and German for reasons that he explains elsewhere, Kant writes: "Art is distinguished from nature as doing [*Tun, facere*] is from acting [*Handeln*] [and in the passage that I quoted just now, so close to the 8th Thesis, it is by means of a passage to practice, as it is translated into French, that is to say to *Tun* and *Handeln* at the same time: doing (art and acting cf. nature)] or producing in general [*wirken, agere*], and the product [*Produkt*] or consequence of the former is distinguished as a work [*Werk, opus*] from the latter as an effect [*Wirkung, effectus*]."[28]

I said at the beginning of this session, and this is what led us on such a long detour, that the statement of the 8th Thesis could be found elsewhere in the same form yet *seem to mean something completely different*; that the unity required by a rationality that is in itself neither simply theoretical nor simply practical, or that is both at the same time, could be found elsewhere while seeming to mean something completely different. For example, I said, in Kant (as we have just sensed) and in Husserl. I won't make the same detour through Husserl but will just note that for this other transcendental idealism that seems to say the same thing as Kant and Marx, and that also makes of teleology the unity between theory and practice, if reason is prior to the opposition between theory and practice, if it is neither simply one nor the other, it is better represented by the theoretical than by the practical, and perhaps in that Husserl is more theoreticist than Kant and—perhaps also, in another sense—than Marx. Every practical utterance can be reduced, reconstituted as a judgment of a theoretical type, says Husserl, let's say, to summarize in a cursory manner a complex machinery and a procedure that I tried to analyze in *Edmund Husserl's "Origin of Geometry": An Introduction*, and in an article that was collected in *Margins* entitled "Form and Meaning."[29] To save time I'll have to refer you to them. Here is just one quotation from Husserl to situate things, very quickly: "Reason allows for no differentiation into 'theoretical,' 'practical,' 'aesthetic' . . . being human is teleological being and an ought-to-be" ("Philosophy as Mankind's

---

28. Immanuel Kant, *Critique of the Power of Judgment*, trans. Paul Guyer and Eric Matthews (Cambridge: Cambridge University Press, 2000), 182.

29. Jacques Derrida, *Edmund Husserl's "Origin of Geometry": An Introduction*, trans. John P. Leavey, Jr. (Lincoln: University of Nebraska Press, 1978); *Margins of Philosophy*, trans. Alan Bass (Chicago: University of Chicago Press, 1982).

Self-Reflection," quoted and commented on in *Origin of Geometry* p. 149; see also Husserl, *Cartesian Meditations* §41).[30]

I come back to the 8th Thesis, that is to the epigraph to Althusser's text "On the Materialist Dialectic," which we unfortunately haven't been able to begin reading today (but we will next time). As I was saying, this 8th Thesis is less practicist than it seems. It imposes very rigorous conditions on its practicism. There are, I was saying, two signs of that. The first, as we have seen, is that practice has to provide a rational solution to theoretical mysticism and to a negative consequence of the theoretical; it is therefore a matter of correcting the theoretical rather than abandoning it, and of correcting it rationally, the value of reason here being the last recourse. The second sign, which we haven't yet broached: it isn't only practice that provides this solution of rational resolution, it is the *Begreifen dieser Praxis*, the conceptual comprehension of this practice, the concept of this practice. This last precision clearly underscores the theoretical, if not theoreticist circumspection with which Marx surrounds his call back to practice. It is doubtless this theoretician [*théoricienne*] insistence, this call back to theoretical rigor within the call to practice that Althusser wanted to emphasize, mark, remark, at the opening of this text that he will later judge still too theoreticist, but which was produced in a situation or context where "theoreticist deviation," as he will call it some years later, had some explaining to do; just as it had some explaining to do concerning the 8th Thesis, which has such a deviation within it, as we have seen, but not by chance and taking into account the general historical and political contextuality that I spoke of at the beginning.

For those who have the patience to stay a few moments longer or who need to laugh a little following this serious journey [*traversée*] through Kant, here is a text precisely on laughter or derision.

We worked today on the inductors *pra*, *par* [by], *tra* (tra as in trans, transformation, traverse, trajectory, etc.) inasmuch as they marked a practical gesture (on the part of the body), a body that no longer lets itself be dominated by the status of the senses that Hegel called theoretical (hearing and sight) in opposition to the practical senses (touch for example, and everything one does with the skin and hands). What relation is there between laughter, derision and *par*, *pra*, *tra*, the body sex, practice, etc.? I'll let a hilarious text by Jean-Pierre Brisset tell us. It is only such a delirious practice that can have

---

30. Cf. Derrida, *"Origin of Geometry": An Introduction*, 136n; Edmund Husserl, *Cartesian Meditations*, trans. Dorion Cairns (Leiden: Martinus Nijhoff, 1977).

us understand the limits of this reason in general that has been keeping us busy for the last two hours. I also want to have you think whether perhaps the practice isn't as delirious as all that. You remember the recourse we had last to it last year, concerning sex and the question "what is it?" in the "Life Death" seminar.[31] Here is my last word for today (I'll first refer you to a book that has just been published, *La Tour de Babil* by Michel Pierssens, who, in a chapter on Brisset, analyzes what he thinks he can determine to be the phallogocentrism that shows through Brisset's philologico-etymological delirium).[32] Here, then: read pp. 111–14.[33] I read these pages, of course, to put you "on guard" against the philologico-etymological precipitation that leads one to think that it suffices to analyze the words theory/practice to deal with the problems, or, more serious still, that one can improvise unwittingly [*sans savoir*] such a semantico-etymological analysis. But in the end, if one must be put on guard against delirium one must also know how to laugh at such warnings [*mises en garde*], and even to laugh at knowing how to laugh, to laugh without knowing.

---

31. In Session 5 of the 1975–76 "Life Death" seminar, Derrida poses this question concerning sexuality in the context of an analysis of François Jacob that follows the discussion of Marx and the concept of production.

32. Michel Pierrsens, *The Power of Babel: A Study of Logophilia*, trans. Carl R. Lovitt (London: Routledge and Kegan Paul, 1980), 90–108.

33. Derrida's reference is to Jean-Pierre Brisset, *La Grammaire logique, suivi de La Science de Dieu* (Paris: Tchou, 1970). [Translator's Note]: Marks in his copy of that text appear to indicate that he read from the fourth new paragraph on p. 111 ("Depuis le jour où les dieux ont goûté à la chair") to the beginning of the second new paragraph on p. 113 ("L'histoire de la femme est écrite dans son nom"); and from the final paragraph of p. 113 ("Nous avons assez analysé de racines") to the end of the second paragraph on p. 114 ("Nous écrivons sous son inspiration pour le trouver").

THIRD SESSION[1]

I'm going to carry on from last time without any recap or transition, feeling justified all the more by my having had to give a quite detailed account of our previous trajectory last time. Without, then, having to situate and justify the need to question, from our point of view here, Althusser's itinerary, and to mark in it the three points of reference that I announced, I'll start out again from the text whose epigraph incited us, a fortnight ago, to take a long detour, namely "On the Materialist Dialectic (On the Unevenness of Origins)" (from 1963, reprinted in *Pour Marx*, 1965). This text, like all those collected in *For Marx*, does not have as its final aim Marxism's passage beyond philosophy. On the contrary, the point is to work on the as yet insufficient, inconsistent elaboration of Marxist philosophy. That is why I am placing this reading here, for you will remember, for me it is about posing the question of what happens *in philosophy*, on the inner edge of philosophy, when one endows the theory/practice pair with major functions, as Marxist practical-theoretical "philosophy" does today. And what I want to dwell on is this Marxist philosophical project, common in the end to Gramsci and Althusser (you remember Gramsci's critique of Croce on this point). We'll later see how Althusser's gesture nevertheless also includes a critique of Gramsci. Althusser's philosophical project during that period is clearly staked out in the preface to *For Marx*. Rest assured, we won't spend two hours on this preface as we did two weeks ago on the epigraph. I'll let you read it. I'll simply point out how Althusser puts on trial there, and provides a panoptical history of all those Marxists who, or Marxisms that faced the temptation of the "end of philosophy," which, he says, was "encouraged by some enigmatically clear texts in Marx's Early Works (1840–45)" and by

---

1. [Translator's Note]: The following handwritten marginal addition is made at the beginning of this session: "<illegible words> announce shorter session, as was decided, I can be interrupted."

what he calls at that moment "Marx's break (1845)" (*For Marx*, 28). Some saw the end of philosophy in action (practice, therefore), in the political realization of philosophy. They referred precisely to the 11th thesis. So, what does Althusser say about this 11th thesis—*Die Philosophen haben die Welt nur verschieden interpretiert, es kömmt darauf an, sie zu verändern*? What does he say about it in his preface? He devotes a single sentence to it, in passing, but it is very loaded, and the weight of it causes us to better understand why the 8th thesis is placed as the epigraph of the text that we are going to study today, rather than the famous 11th thesis. It all looks as if, against the reigning prejudice, Althusser judged the 8th thesis to be more surely and more rigorously Marxist, better protected against ambiguity than the famous 11th one. And that isn't so astonishing to us since we recognized, two weeks ago, the theoretician [*théoricienne*] insistence of the 8th thesis, and all the rational, theoretical and conceptual safeguards (we recognized those three elements) that it placed around the value of "practice." Since Althusser was especially concerned at that time with recalling Marxism to its theoretical rigor it was to be expected that he would privilege, as it were, the 8th thesis over the 11th, and that is one of the reasons why I insisted on that last time. What then does Althusser say about the 11th thesis in such a loaded clause? He says that the language of the 11th thesis is "theoretically ambiguous." And in the following sentence, that this ambiguity, this theoretical ambiguity leads to "theoretical pragmatism." I'll read it—so it operates within this history, this putting an era of French Marxism on trial—"the most militant and the most generous tended towards an interpretation of the 'end of philosophy' as its 'realization' and celebrated the death of philosophy in action, in its political realization and proletarian consumption, unreservedly endorsing the famous Thesis on Feuerbach which, in ambiguous theoretical language, counterposes the transformation of the world to its interpretation. It was, *and always will be*, only a short step from there to theoretical pragmatism" (ibid.).

In other words, through its ambiguity, the 11th thesis, which breaks down even the theoretical or theoreticist guardrails of the 8th thesis, leads to theoretical pragmatism.

What does that mean? That one is going to have to arm theory against pragmatism, but since Marxism couldn't be a simple theoreticist theory—that would be a bit much—that one is going to have to arm theoretical practice against theoretical pragmatism and bring out the theoretical and practical conditions of a non-pragmatic practice, a non-pragmatic theoretical practice. What is theoretical pragmatism? What is the difference between practice and pragmatics?

The words are very close, obviously, which is what makes the question interesting, and if the pragmatic is, from a Marxist point of view, a corruption or, if you prefer, a deviation from practice, from what practice must be, from good practice, then we have every reason to make a clear distinction between practice and pragmatics. An etymological dictionary won't be much help to us, it won't provide decisive assistance in any case, first because *praktikos* and *pragmatikos* are so close to each other in their origins and in their Greek usage; second because the history of the progressive displacements of the pragmatic, of the sedimentation of senses and usages that was formed in it, is what will contribute—even insufficiently—to rendering intelligible to us the emergence of this near opposition, within the context that we are currently studying, between practical value and pragmatic value. Moreover, it would be very useful (of pragmatic value, precisely) if someone here were to take on a presentation concerning the formation of the concept of the pragmatic through history, through to its sense in Kant, its juridical and ecclesiastical senses, and in the American philosophy that bears the name of pragmatism, etc., including of course the pejorative connotation that can be given to it, in particular in revolutionary Marxist strategy.

I'll open here an anticipatory parenthesis. Moreover, it is also to anticipate anticipation, which in a moment will become an indispensable concept. An anticipatory parenthesis that anticipates the moment, should we ever get there, when we'll reach the second emphasis or inflection of "it must be done," the one which, insisting on the "must," but a "must" that impels one to accomplish only by transgressing a law, a prohibition, a limit in any case—by exceeding—stands in relation to something like the law, right, the ethico-juridical, and constitutes the operation of "doing" as a necessarily juridical structure, I mean one traversed by a judicial process even and especially into transgression. The fact of doing is structurally, and not accidentally, transfixed by law, by a relation to the law. Fact[2] or doing [*faire*] is no more foreign to whomever declares the law or what the law declares than is the thing [*chose*] foreign to the cause (*causa*: legal proceeding, matter to be dealt with, debate, lawsuit). I'd like to pause on this essentially *litigious* character of the pragmatic for a moment. *Pragmatikos* most often designates, in Greek, whatever concerns action, what is proper to action, a *pragmatikos* man is one capable of acting, and more precisely in business, and more precisely in political or legal business, jurisprudence, that is to say concerning a law where the case, the differential singularity of each case is

---

2. [Translator's Note]: *fait*, also "what is done."

taken into account. The case, juridico-political casuistry, the differentiality of causes or affairs, the prudence of jurisprudence, that is where *pragmatikos* resides. As a result one can foresee the sense that will regularly come to be attached in current parlance to the words "pragmatic" or "pragmatism": empiricism, opportunism, utilitarianism or unmediated realism, prudence but a *providentia* that does not look very far ahead of itself, a shortsighted prudence, one that wants to see only the particular case that it has before it, in its proper difference, without being interested in the concept of this case, a providence or a prudence that foresees only in a shortsighted way (absence of an objectifying lens), which therefore precipitates or improvises rather than anticipates. But naturally if empiricism—as attention to differentiality—which haunts pragmatism, is or can be discredited, it can also turn that objection back against the concept, against theoretical responsibility, against the desire to anticipate absolutely, and criticize its inattention to difference, its erasure of difference and contemplative delay, the tendency to wait and see, theoreticist suspension. What I was wanting to insist on within this anticipatory or suspensive parenthesis is the fact that *pragma*, this time—and not only what is pragmatic—*pragma* is translated as thing, affair, what one does or the action of doing, the doing of "must be done," it isn't a doing or thing that is neutral or natural, pre-predicative, if you wish, precultural or presymbolic. *Pragma* is already a doing [*faire*] or an affair that is engaged in a proceeding, it is a thing in process, *Sache* in German (in contrast to *Ding*), or *causa*, cause as object of a legal proceeding, of a debate, a decision to be taken, a judgment or sentence taking effect and not remaining theoretical. It is a thing as correlative to a non-theoretical practice if you wish. It is an affair, something that matters. In the end, a quite good translation of *es kommt drauf an* in the 11th thesis would be: what is important—the affair, as *to be done* [*à-faire*], as law—is to change the world. The idea of law, of the imperative, of prescription, of debt is thus inscribed in *pragma*; "it must" is inscribed in this doing. And the juridico-political determination of "it must" weighed from the start on the sense of *pragma*, and of *pragmatic*, in Greek and in Latin, in Latin where it was able to follow a very precisely juridical direction, designating sometimes, very strictly, a rule (and there you can see a prescriptive "it must" intervene in the pragmatic itself), the rule of civil power in ecclesiastical matters. There is for example a pragmatics of Saint-Louis (Louis IX) who rules over the institution of the Gallican Church, gives back to the Gallican Church its rights vis-à-vis Rome, etc., etc. I close this parenthesis and come back to Althusser's text, to that point in the preface to *For Marx* where it is a question of those French Marxists who had celebrated the end of philosophy as political realization by referring to this 11th thesis that "in ambiguous theoretical language, counterposes the transformation of the world to its interpretation. It was, *and always will be*, only a short step from there to theoretical pragmatism" (*For Marx*, 28).

Notice that Althusser, underlining the present of the formula "it is always only a short step," indeed intends, at the moment he intervenes, to take a position in a current, determinate situation, in relation to current political effects. That is important if we are to read this text appropriately. Next, note how the 11th thesis is evaluated for its theoretical statement or content: its theoretical content is what is ambiguous and judged as such. It is therefore in the name of a theoretical reading of an utterance considered, from this point of view, theoretical, that this evaluation is made; it evaluates the theoretical ambiguity of the 11th thesis. The question that isn't posed here—it is in any case judged in the context in which Althusser takes a position and intervenes—is whether this 11th thesis is important for its theoretical content or not, whether its enunciative status, its structure as discursive event does or does not belong to the category of theoretical or philosophical "utterance," or whether, precisely by means of what it says it prescribes another mode of reading. Note finally that the pragmatism that is denounced as a deleterious, politically harmful effect of this headlong rush toward death of philosophy, in making a religion of the 11th thesis and its theoretically ambiguous content, this pragmatism that is denounced (empiricism, opportunism, tacticism without strategy, improvisation, relativist casuistry, etc.), the pragmatism that is denounced is a theoretical pragmatism, occurring within theory. Not only *activist* pragmatism, cf. above, p. 27, "political activism." It is plasticity or theoretical empiricism devoid of principle, rigor and specificity, the adaptation of the theoretical to the immediate facts on the ground, those of the theoretical or political situation. One might say that Althusser condemns theoretical pragmatism as a harmful effect of the simplified practicism that some presumed to uncover in the 11th thesis, somewhat in the same way that, according to the 8th thesis, mysticism was presumed to be a deleterious effect of theory or of theoretical isolation, of theory speculating outside of practice. In the same way that theory speculating outside of practice ends in mysticism, so practice without theoretical—here, philosophical—rigor, practice within the horizon of the death of philosophy would be pragmatism. Pragmatism would be the degenerate form of the practical imperative, but here Althusser *primarily* takes to task theoretical pragmatism. The analogy that I drew between the mystical effect of theory (identified in the 8th thesis) and theoretical pragmatism, both of them being harmful, degenerative effects, that analogy finds its confirmation in the fact that a little further down Althusser leads one to think that the Marxist philosophers who believed in the end of philosophy and its political realization continued to make philosophy, as completed/fulfilled by politics, their religion. That's what Althusser calls the pragmatico-religious death of philosophy; the other death, the other model of the death of philosophy, during those years, had taken on rather a form or norm of scientific positivism: philosophy replaced/fulfilled by science. But these two deaths, Althusser then says, pragmatico-religious death and positivist death are not really *"philosophical* deaths of philosophy." Whence a third current that also found its reference in Marx (*Capital* this time), a *critical* current, that of philosophy as critique of "ideological reveries," "ideological illusion," "ideological phantasms," ideology there being determined as illusion, reverie, phantasm (a problem that I leave aside for the moment). A still "mythical" hope, Althusser says, that "will achieve its philosophical end in the living death of a critical consciousness" (30).

These three forms of failure (pragmatico-religious, positivist, criticist), which were also three philosophical dogmatisms, three dogmatisms concerning the end of philosophy, are said to belong to the period of Stalinist dogmatism. But the end of that period hasn't made them disappear in one fell swoop. And so Althusser's point—in this precise situation of a nascent post-Stalinism, of the end of Stalinist dogmatism—is not to think the end or death of philosophy otherwise, but to reconfigure Marxist philosophy *itself*, and not even to re-configure it, but to configure it, for it is still to come. And that is why (in situating how I'm developing things at this moment) I spoke of the inner edge of philosophy: it is a question, still, of constructing a philosophy, philosophy, and Marxism must be a or *the* philosophy. At this point, from this point of view, Althusser is, at least in what he says, therefore analogous to Gramsci in his argument with Croce: Marxism is not the death, the suppression of philosophy and its simple replacement by revolutionary practice, it is a new philosophy of praxis, yet to be configured, still to come on the basis of a previously existing foundation. And that is indeed Althusser's conclusion at the end of part I of this preface entitled "Today": Marxist philosophy is *founded*, but in an *undeveloped* state; it must be elaborated and given *theoretical existence and consistency* (cf. 31). And the language that Althusser employs to speak of this task is indeed that of philosophy speaking of its own edification, its own construction, like that of a systematic and founded architecture.[3] The architectonic project—the proj-

---

3. [Translator's Note]: A partially legible handwritten marginal addition appears here to state, "Deconstruction doesn't deconstruct down to the ground [*fondement*]

ect of a system with its building, fundamental, foundational metaphor is literally present at the moment when Althusser recalls that Marxism is, must be philosophical. And if you remember what we were reading in Kant last time, namely that reason, the interest of human reason is, in its nature, "architectonic, i.e., it considers all cognitions [*connaissances*] as belonging to a possible system,"[4] well then the Marxist philosophical project as it appears here—for example in the passage that I am going to read—is eminently philosophical and partakes of rationality in its most continuous element, of the interest of reason in its most profound permanence. Here is what Althusser writes at the end of chapter I of "Today": "The end of dogmatism puts us face to face with this reality: that Marxist philosophy, founded by Marx in the very act of founding his theory of history, has still largely [*en grande partie*] to be constituted, since, as Lenin said, only the cornerstones have been laid down; that the theoretical difficulties we debated in the dogmatist night were not completely [*de part en part*] artificial—rather they were largely the result of a meagerly elaborated Marxist philosophy; or better, that in the rigid caricatural forms we suffered and maintained, including the theoretical monstrosity of the two sciences [proletarian and bourgeoise], something of an unsettled problem was really present in grotesque and blind forms—the writings of theoretical Leftism (the young Lukács and Korsch) which have finally been republished are a sufficient witness to this; and finally, that our lot and our duty today is quite simply to pose and confront those problems in the light of day, if Marxist philosophy is to be given some existence or a little theoretical consistency" (30–31).

Those final words must be heard very precisely and rigorously, and in line with what their syntax makes clear. To give a theoretical consistency to Marxist philosophy doesn't simply mean that there is—or must be—a Marxist philosophy to be constructed or elaborated, that Marxist philosophy is a *constructum* to come; it also means that Marxist philosophical construction must have theoretical consistency, in other words that the theoretical recourse is the principal one, the tribunal of last resort for judging the philosophical character of philosophy. The theoretical is no longer one aspect, one side, a determination of the philosophical, but the opposite. The philosophical appears before the theoretical tribunal and constitutes a region of the theoretical, of the theoretical in general, or of theoretical practice in general. It is not this little sentence alone that attests to that, in which case I wouldn't

---

<illegible word>; it deconstructs the motif of ground and the architectonic schema, it questions it."

4. Kant, *Pure Reason*, 502.

draw your attention to it, but a whole general movement that I would like to bring to light today: what we have here is not an inflection of the philosophical, of the rational philosophical constructum, an inflection of the architectonic toward its theoretical side, toward the theoretical form of interest (what can I know rather than what should I do or what may I hope?), but a subordination of the philosophical as a whole to a theoretical instance or criteriology. The immediate confirmation of this displacement making philosophy a dependency, I would say almost a regional dependency of theory in general, of a theory in general that exceeds philosophy and can't be reduced to it, not being essentially philosophical, the immediate confirmation can be found in some other reference elements that I'll point out to you. First, p. 25 of the same text, at the moment when some elements of explanation concerning the poverty of French philosophy since the Revolution are given, the sole exception being Auguste Comte, "the only mind worthy of interest that it produced," and whom French philosophy went after with a vengeance. In the course of this history painted with a broad brush, Althusser emphasizes that what characterizes this French tradition is on the one hand a certain tradition of the political and the primacy of the political accompanied by "a certain failure to appreciate the role of theory," and, he specifies, "particularly *philosophical* theory as opposed to political and economic theory" (26). In other words philosophy is one of the forms of theory; there is political theory, economic theory, theories of various sciences, etc., and there is philosophical theory. And a little further along Althusser regrets the absence, within all this history, of real "masters" of philosophy, and of Marxist philosophy (the word "masters" appears four times), and the paucity, I am quoting, of "men of sufficient *philosophical* formation to realize that Marxism should not be simply a political doctrine, a 'method' of analysis and action, but also, over and above the rest, the *theoretical domain of a fundamental investigation*, indispensable not only to the development of the science of society and of the various 'human sciences,' but also to that of the natural sciences and philosophy" (ibid.). Marxism—as theoretical domain of a fundamental investigation upon which would depend as branches, regions, or secondary zones, not only the social or human sciences and the sciences of nature but also philosophy—represents a displacement that is remarkable and, to my knowledge, absolutely new in the history of philosophy. I mean by that that at the very moment when the project of Marxist philosophy is being relaunched, against the theme of the end of philosophy, at the moment when Marxism is being opened to elaboration as philosophy and the discourse is being proffered from the point of view of rational-philosophical interest, at that precise moment two gestures intersect along the lines of a very strange trajectory that seems to me to be as follows: one gesture consists in repeating the most fundamentally traditional philosophical movement, namely subordinating to a single fundamental and general instance the totality of regions of theoretical knowledge and practical knowledge (natural and human sciences, political sciences, etc.). That is the gesture that every philosophy, from Plato and Aristotle to Hegel and Husserl, has incessantly reproduced. A general, fundamental science (here metaphysics, or first philosophy, there *metaphysica generalis*, the science of logic, elsewhere general or fundamental ontology) as thinking of being in general or objectivity in general subordinates districts or regions for which it remains the last recourse, the ultimate jurisdiction. This project, this gesture—which represents the most constant and, one might say, the most authentically philosophical tradition—is taken under its wing by Marxism as Althusser conceives it, and whose philosophical relaunching he is in fact proposing. But this solidly classical gesture is strangely disturbed, derailed, hijacked, if one can say, displaced by another (blackboard). This other one is, I would say, only half-traditional. It isn't traditional at all to the extent that now the fundamental recourse is represented no longer by philosophy but by theory, the "theoretical domain of a fundamental investigation." In other words, theory is substituted for philosophy, which becomes a dependent zone alongside other particular sciences (of society or of nature). Such a gesture would no doubt have been considered monstrous by classical philosophers judging the demotion of philosophy to the rank of a regional discipline to be impossible or absurd; they would have deemed it impossible or absurd unless they were to find a way out by suggesting that in fact a purely verbal substitution has been effected and that in fact the authentic philosophical instance, as project worthy of itself, continues to be represented by what Althusser is calling the "theoretical domain of a fundamental investigation," there remaining the question of knowing what could still be put under the rubric of "philosophy" once it had been made into a regional discipline. A philosophy as regional discipline would be a contradiction in terms. But this strangely displacing and substitutive gesture rejoins all the same a philosophical tradition that can recognize itself in it when the fundamental instance that it places in place of philosophy is the theoretical, theoreticist instance and not any other. Now, with the exception perhaps of Kant (which is why from the start I reserved a place for Kant in this story), each time that a philosopher defined the fundamental instance of first philosophy or fundamental or general ontology, the theoretical held the dominant position.

Another confirmation of the theoretical as ultimate general, non-regional jurisdiction not only of the other sciences but of a regionalized philosophy, is found at the beginning of the second chapter of "Today." While recognizing that his earlier text "On the Young Marx" (also republished in *For Marx*) still belonged too much to what Althusser had just defined as the "myth of critical philosophy," he declares that that text contained an essential question. Now this essential question is that of Marxist philosophy's right to philosophical existence, that right to philosophical existence being qualified here as a theoretical right. The juridical instance that decides whether Marxist philosophy does or doesn't have a right to exist is not properly philosophical but theoretical, a theoretical jurisdiction. Here, then, the theoretical is placed above, or before and independently of the philosophical as such. I'll read (p. 31): "The piece on the Young Marx is still trapped in the myth of an evanescent critical philosophy. Nevertheless, it does contain *the* essential *question*, irresistibly drawn from us by our trials, failures and impotence: [underscored from here on] *What is Marxist philosophy? Has it any theoretical right to existence? And if it does exist by right* [by theoretical right, therefore], *how can its specificity be defined?* This essential question was raised practically by another, apparently historical but really theoretical question: the question of reading and interpreting Marx's Early Works."

This positioning of the question reminds us in passing—I'll just note this—of the link that there has always been, essentially, between the question of right and the question in theoretical form. Before even being a question of theoretical right, the question of right in itself, as a de jure question, is in essence theoretical. And inasmuch as the question of right is not one question among others for philosophy you can see to what extent it ties the philosophical to the theoretical.

Now, saying that there is and must be a Marxist philosophy, and that its right to existence must be theoretical, does not necessarily reinscribe the specific content of Marxist philosophy within the tradition, even if its affiliation with the philosophical tradition as such is maintained. What then is the specificity of Marxist philosophy? The reading of Marx's works and the concept of an epistemological break—concerning which Althusser recalls how and why he had imported it from Bachelard (I'll leave aside the problems relating to that importation) in order to uncover in Marx's trajectory a rupture that allowed for "the emergence of a new conception of philosophy" (32)—the reading framework recalled here by Althusser brings to light and confirms that it is indeed a theoretical demarcation, namely what leads to science, the passage from "a pre-scientific problematic to a scientific problematic," it is indeed a theoretico-epistemological problematic that decides not only the theoretical right to philosophy but the specificity of the Marxist conception of philosophy. Two consequences follow: the very concepts that underwrite this reading of Marx and this demarcation within his corpus, these two concepts, namely that of problematic (Jacques Martin) and that of epistemological break (Bachelard) would already have been in Marx but, as Althusser says, raising as a result an enormous problem that I'll simply point to, "in the practical state" (32) [comment].

Second consequence: if there is an epistemological break within Marx's corpus, differentiating a before from an after, prescientific from scientific, then specifically Marxist philosophy must be found after the break; and hence the "Theses on Feuerbach" that serve here as our main thread (for this phase of the seminar) are placed by Althusser before the break, but just before, on what he calls the "extreme earlier limit [*le bord anterieur extrême*] of this break." According to Althusser that would explain their ambiguity, which we were talking about earlier, their theoretical ambiguity. They are ambiguous because, if they are not yet beyond the break, nor are they simply on this side of it, but on the edge, the extreme earlier edge. The break itself is for Althusser (at least at this moment in his trajectory: I remind you that it is a trajectory that we are studying and for the moment we are within the internal analysis of its first stage), the break itself is deemed by Althusser to be unequivocal. He writes: "There is an unequivocal '*epistemological break*' in Marx's work which does in fact occur at the point where Marx himself locates it, in the book, unpublished in his lifetime, which is a critique of his erstwhile philosophical (ideological) consciousness: *The German Ideology* [comment: erstwhile philosophical/ideological consciousness]. The 'Theses on Feuerbach,' which are only a few sentences long, mark out the extreme earlier limit of this break, the point at which the new theoretical consciousness is already beginning to show through in the erstwhile consciousness and the erstwhile language, that is, as formulae and *concepts that are necessarily ambiguous and unbalanced*" (33). [Comment: the equivocality, the teleology of "already," the dominant epistemo-theoretical recourse: not positivist, but ...⁵].

Finally, last confirmation before coming to the text "On the Materialist Dialectic," last confirmation of the fact that it is indeed a question of a foundation and a philosophical construction, a philosophical architectonic that is being inscribed—I insist on this—two times, in two places, on two levels, that of theory in general, which occupies the place of philosophy in the (transcendental or ontological) tradition, and that of philosophy as one region among others within the theoretical—last confirmation, then, of this philosophical fact in "On the Materialist Dialectic,"⁶ what I will call philosophical self-responsibility.

---

5. [Translator's Note]: Ellipsis in typescript.
6. Seemingly incorrect attribution: Derrida means to refer to the Preface to *For Marx*.

The demand for self-responsibility is an essential trait of philosophy. What is it? Well, the requirement that it be able to respond, to give an account and explain the reason, not simply for the principles and bases or conditions of possibility of other discourses, of the other regions of knowledge, but also and in the first place for itself. Well, this trait occurs, and not by chance, and even with the figure of an essential circularity if not specularity that characterizes this schema of self-affirmation and self-responsibility. It appears in the text that concerns us at the moment when it is a question of underscoring the essential stakes in the reading of Marx. This reading is possible only on the basis of Marx, that is to say it has to be admitted that Marx provides the "theoretical concepts" that alone allow for reading him and notably for reading the epistemological break that marks his text. A Marxist theory of the (differential) nature of theoretical formations and of their history must be what allows for the reading of this theoretical formation that is Marxism or the text of Marx. This "theory of epistemological history," Althusser then says, is "Marxist philosophy itself" (*For Marx*, 38). As for the circle requiring that in order to read properly a theoretical formation such as Marx's text one must first inherit from it a theory of theoretical formations, Althusser calls it "indispensable," the "dialectical circle" of a question asked of the object concerning its nature that operates "on the basis of a theoretical problematic [anticipation] which in putting its object to the test puts itself to the test of its object [pro-anticipation]" etc. (ibid.). And this dialectical circle of self-responsibility, *qua* dialectic, is precisely what attests to the philosophical value of the process, what distinguishes for example, in the very interior of Marxism, the science of history (historical materialism) from dialectical materialism as philosophy. It is this circle of self-foundation and self-responsibility that defines the philosophical as such. In that sense the gesture proposed by Althusser is, in its formal schema at least—but the formal schema is here that of the essential predicate by which one recognizes that a philosophy is a philosophy—is thus in its formal schema the gesture of philosophy speaking of itself and positing itself as philosophy. In a certain way Althusser accepts that; he says it *but* while he is at the same time saying in the end that Marxism is a philosophy that, like all philosophy, lays claim to self-responsibility (giving an account of itself); he specifies that it is the sole or first philosophy really to face this test, and to face it—this is the specific difference that I am drawing your attention to—to confront it *theoretically*. In other words the least apparent paradox is that it is the theoretical that, as such, distinguishes between traditional philosophies and Marxist philosophy. The theoretical is thus once again placed in the position of an arbiter—as it were above the philosophical at the very moment when Marxism is positing itself as a philosophy; it is the theoretical that decides by right whether a philosophy is indeed a philosophy and whether it stands up in the way it should, that is theoretically, to the test of self-responsibility. In other words giving an account of itself, answering for itself is a gesture that, for philosophy, must be a gesture that is in the final analysis theoretical, and Marxism would be the only philosophy that answers for itself theoretically, before the theoretical tribunal. I'll now read the passage that I just referred to, it is still in "Today," near the end (p. 38):

> But the circle implied by this operation is, like all circles of this kind, simply the dialectical circle of the question asked of an object as to its nature, on the basis of a theoretical problematic which in putting its object to the test puts itself to the test of its object. That Marxism can and must itself be the object of the epistemological question, that this epistemological question can only be asked as a function of the Marxist theoretical problematic, that is necessity itself for a theory which defines itself dialectically, not merely as a science of history (historical materialism) but also and simultaneously as a philosophy, a philosophy that is capable of accounting for the nature of theoretical formations and their history, and therefore *capable of accounting for itself*, by taking itself as its own object. Marxism is the only philosophy that theoretically faces up to this test. (38–39).

Of course I underline the word "theoretically." A test [*épreuve*],[7] an experience is always practical, always has something of a practical traverse, a trajectory, a traversing-traversed becoming. Every philosophy puts itself to the test of circular self-responsibility, every philosophy practices or tries to practice the test of the self-reflexive circle that consists in taking itself for its object. Althusser implicitly recognizes that every philosophy puts itself to that test. But "Marxism is the only philosophy that theoretically faces up to this test." Contrary to those who might have thought that the primacy of practice is what distinguishes Marxist philosophy from every other philosophy, Althusser, at least at this moment in his trajectory, finds the very *distinction* of Marxism in the theoretical.

And that is why sometimes the theoretical is positioned above the philosophical as a last recourse (occupying in a way—schematically—the place of reason in general as we recognized last time) that declares philosophical right, the right of a philosophy to declare itself as such, and sometimes the theoretical merges purely and simply with the philosophical, as for example in this last paragraph of "Today":

---

7. Derrida places a hand-drawn frame around each occurrence of this word in the preceding quote and in this paragraph.

This work which is essential to a *reading* of Marx is, in the strict sense, simultaneously the work of theoretical elaboration of Marxist philosophy. A theory which enables us to see clearly in Marx, to distinguish science from ideology, to deal with the difference between them within the historical relation between them and to deal with the discontinuity of the epistemological break within the continuity of a historical process; a theory which makes it possible to distinguish a word from a concept, to distinguish the existence or non-existence of a concept behind a word, to discern the existence of a concept by a word's function in the theoretical discourse, to define the nature of a concept by its function in the problematic, and thus by the location it occupies in the system of the "theory"; this theory which alone makes possible an authentic reading of Marx's writings, a reading which is both epistemological and historical, this theory is in fact nothing other than Marxist philosophy itself. (39)[8]

If every theory (let's give it a small "t") is now, as "On the Materialist Dialectic" will say, a specific form of practice, if then theory is that form of practice called theoretical practice, with the result that the primacy of first or last recourse comes down to practice, how is one to explain the use of a capital, such that, after reminding us that every theory was a specification of practice, a theoretical practice, Althusser proposes calling Theory, with a capital "T," the Theory of practice in general, namely the materialist dialectic (repeat and explain). That is what we'll try to understand next time by broaching that text—this time, I promise—having been waylaid or diverted here first on the immediate threshold of its epigraph, and second on the further removed preamble of a preface. That text, I remind you, still belongs to the first moment of what I've called Althusser's trajectory. If the *tra*, if the idea of the trajectory belongs, as we said, to the value of *practice*, it is indeed a matter of practice; and if the idea of a test, of putting to the test is the idea of practice itself, then we shall have to see how, in Althusser's trajectory, the proposition that it is the theoretical character of the test faced that distinguishes Marxist philosophy, is put to the test. The text that we'll read next time, and which belongs to the same set as "Today," clearly confirms the position taken by capitalizing Theory. We shall have to see how the capitalized Theoretical stands up to the test.

---

8. [Translator's Note]: Penultimate paragraph in English translation.

FOURTH SESSION

Within a problematic framework that I won't go back over we found it necessary to pose the question of the investment by something like a Marxist philosophical project in the theory/practice pair, having read that first in Gramsci and Althusser. During the previous two sessions we began, through a more or less direct reading of the epigraph to "On the Materialist Dialectic" and of the preface to *For Marx*, to put into perspective what I called, not without explanation, Althusser's trajectory. I won't repeat, not even in the form of a summary, what was said from that point of view, but will take up what I'd be tempted to define as a first state or first stage.

Naturally, we will not be concerned here with producing the history, of producing the history of Althusser's discourse or practice, for two reasons. First, of course, because that history is still in process. It hasn't come to an end. And I would say that that is so almost by definition when it comes to a Marxist philosophical practice. Next, because my point is not itself historical and certainly not in the sense of producing the history of philosophy or the history of doctrines, but in the sense of determining the forces or stakes invested in "theory/practice," determining them in a mode where it remains a matter of knowing whether that mode is practical and/or theoretical.

For example, through the *situation* of the first state or first stage we can separate out certain essential predicates of the Marxist determination of practice—production and transformation or the labor of transformation—that will restart our overall problematic and raise other types of questions.

The main thread that I'll be following to situate this first stage will, as directly as possible, be that (naturally one could choose others) of *definitions*, in the form of the explicit definition that Althusser gives, in "On the Materialist Dialectic," of practice, of theory, of theoretical practice and the Theory of practice (*For Marx*, 166–68).

Before getting into the content of these definitions I'll point out at least the originality of the logical configuration, if you wish, within which they are contained. For the practical and theoretical cannot function only as the objects of these definitions, where by "the object of these definitions" I mean what is defined in these definitions. Practice and/or theory are not defined by these definitions; they are implied in the defining of the definition, in the very possibility of the definition. How so?

What leads Althusser to propose these definitions is the following question: what is the specific difference that distinguishes Marxist dialectics from Hegelian dialectics? That comes down to asking oneself—presuming that there must be a Marxist philosophy and that its name is dialectical materialism—what the specificity of Marxist philosophy is. That question *about* the specificity of Marxist philosophy is, Althusser specifies, a "theoretical problem" (*For Marx*, 164), and he thereby confirms, once more, that the ultimate criterion for and on philosophy—the philosophical—is something like the theoretical.

But, Althusser says—and this is where what is defined intervenes in a circular manner (cf. above) in the very conditions of the definition—the theoretical problem and its solution *already* exist. Where do they already exist? What is this "already?" What is the structure of this "already?" This "already" is already determined as "practice," as practical state. These problems and theoretical solutions exist already, Althusser says, in the practice of Marxism, and they exist there in the practical state: "To pose and resolve our theoretical problem ultimately means to express theoretically the *'solution,' existing in the practical state*, that Marxist practice has found for a real difficulty it has encountered in its development, whose existence it has noted, and, according to its own admission, settled" (165). Or again: the solution to a problem *exists* in Marxist practice, "so we only have to express it theoretically" (ibid.), says Althusser. Naturally, there is something tautological about this formula—as if it were simply a matter of expressing, that is of putting into words what was already there in silence, of rendering explicit a practical already-there—and Althusser specifies that this theoretical expression of what was already there in the practical state produces knowledge and critiques an illusion. And it is this concept of the production of a concept or of knowledge that will bear the whole difficulty, already at this level. For theoretical production to mean something other than rendering explicit or bringing to light what was there already, there must be a practical transformation that breaks with this already-there, bringing something new, and as a consequence producing something that wasn't yet in the practical state in the already-there. In any case, the fact that the theoretical produces knowledge that was already there, in the practical state, irreversibly marks the priority, the primordiality of the practical over the theoretical, of the practical state over the theoretical state, a priority that is in excess of itself for it announces already that the theoretical remains a development of the practical, a species of the practical, theoretical practice inasmuch as it produces knowledge that was already there in the practical state.[1] It remains to be understood what purpose this production serves or what is going on with this theoretical production that merely expresses what was already in the practical state. In order to reply to that question—which Althusser asks literally—he will propose the definitions that interest us here. As he writes—and I'll quote it because here also we must be very attentive to the literality of his text:

> And if I am then asked: but what use is there in posing this problem *in theory* if its solution has already existed for a long time in the practical state? why give a theoretical expression to this practical solution, a theoretical solution it has so far done very well without? what do we gain by this "speculative" investigation that we do not possess already?
> One sentence is enough to answer this question: Lenin's "Without theory, no revolutionary practice". Generalizing it: theory is essential to practice, to the practice of which it is the theory as well as the practices that it helps bring to birth or to grow. But the transparency of this sentence is not enough; we must also know what *qualifies it as valid* [ses titres de validité], so we must pose the question: what are we to understand by *theory*, if it is to be essential to *practice*?
> I shall only discuss the aspects of this theme that are indispensable to our investigation. I propose to use the following *definitions*, in the form of preliminary approximations. (166, Translation modified)[2]

Such are the protocols of the definitions that will follow. Three brief remarks on these protocols before getting into the definitions; three more or less secondary remarks, depending on how they are developed.

1. By going back from the end of the protocol toward its beginning: it is always a matter of demanding *qualifications*. Althusser says that if one is to quote Lenin's words "without revolutionary theory, no revolutionary practice," one needs to know what qualifies them as valid. And you know that this demand for credentials, a demand that takes a juridical and juridico-theoretical form

---

1. [Translator's Note]: A handwritten marginal addition here reads: "Fill a gap between theory and practice? p. 165."

2. [Translator's Note]: The translator of *Pour Marx* corrects Althusser's misquotation of Lenin in the above quote, writing "Without revolutionary theory, no revolutionary practice." Cf. *Pour Marx*, 167: "*A cette question, nous pourrions répondre d'un mot, celui de Lénine: 'Sans théorie pas de pratique révolutionnaire.'*" See Derrida's following discussion.

(as I underscored last time), returns regularly in Althusser; it is even an essential basis for the critical questions that he goes on to pose. But later—I'll say justifiably [*à juste titre*]—he will define this type of juridical demand as the ideology that is present in philosophy itself. That poses enormous problems, all the more so because in the note to the 1974 "Elements of Self-Criticism" to which I'm referring Law is said to be "one with ideology" and in that respect it is a unique case (*Essays in Self-Criticism*, 117n12). This note to "Elements of Self-Criticism" that would need to be studied very closely, and which I'll be content simply to read, is not a self-critical note. It aims at philosophers who don't suspect the presence of the Law in philosophy itself.

Read "Elements of Self-Criticism," note on p. 117, and potentially from the beginning of the paragraph on p. 116 ("We therefore have the right, and the duty."):

> One has only to open a textbook of law or jurisprudence, to see clearly that Law [*Droit*]—which, uniquely, works as one with ideology, because it needs it to be able to "function"—and therefore legal ideology, is, in the last instance, and usually surprisingly transparently, the basis of all bourgeois ideology. One needs a Marxist lawyer to demonstrate it, and a Marxist philosopher to understand it. As far as philosophers in general are concerned, they have not yet cut through the fog that surrounds them, and they hardly suspect the presence of the Law and of legal ideology in their ruminations: in philosophy itself. However, the evidence is there: the dominant classical bourgeois philosophy (and its by-products, even the modern ones) is built on legal ideology, and its "philosophical objects" (philosophy has no object, it has *its* objects) are legal categories or entities: the Subject, the Object, Liberty, Free Will, Property (Properties), Representation, Person, Thing, etc. But those thinkers, those Marxists, who have recognized the bourgeois legal character of these categories and who criticize them, must still find their way out of the trap of traps: the idea and programme of a *"theory of knowledge"*. This is the keystone of classical bourgeois philosophy, which is still dominant. Now unless (like Lenin and Mao) we use this expression in a context which indicates *where to get out of the circle*, in the philosophical rather than the scientific sense, then the idea may be taken as constitutive of philosophy, and even of "Marxist philosophy", and you remain caught in bourgeois ideology's trap of traps. For the simple *question* to which the "theory of knowledge" replies is still a *question of Law*, posed in terms of the validity of knowledge. (*Essays in Self-Criticism*, 117n12)

2. Second remark. Lenin's words, which are not themselves clear enough, but in respect of which one must ask what qualifies them as valid, are from Lenin's "What is to be done?" (1901–2), in a subchapter of chapter 1,

subchapter entitled "Engels on the Importance of the Theoretical Struggle" (Lenin had previously criticized Bernstein for the latter's denial of the idea of the "*ultimate aim*," the theory of class struggle and the idea of the dictatorship of the proletariat).[3] In this subchapter on Engels and the importance of the theoretical struggle Lenin recalls, in a situation he considers one of "theoretical disorder," at a time when, he says, "the wide spread of Marxism was accompanied by a certain lowering of the theoretical level"[4] (hence an analogous situation, one of theoretical insufficiency analogous to that diagnosed by Althusser, into which he is intervening). Lenin recalls, then, that Marx's thinking was not to "make 'theoretical' concessions," and he brings that to the attention of those who "seek—in [Marx's] name—to belittle the significance of theory." And it is then that he writes "without revolutionary theory there can be no revolutionary movement,"[5] which is therefore the sentence that Althusser has quoted, or rather translated (no revolutionary practice) or transposed, since he forgets "revolutionary" following "theory." Lenin says: "without revolutionary theory there can be no revolutionary movement"; Althusser: "without theory no revolutionary practice" (cf. *Pour Marx*, 167).[6] But Lenin's sentence will be restored in its entirety on page 52 of *Lenin and Philosophy*, which we'll come to shortly. The rest of Lenin's text will conclude that *"the role of vanguard fighter can be fulfilled only by a party that is guided by the most advanced theory."*[7]

3. Third remark on the protocol of the definitions.

When Althusser notes the need for qualifications he does so in respect of the theoretical statement regarding problems and solutions that are in the practical state. Moving to the theoretical expression of problems and solutions that are in the practical state must be justified; theory's being essential to practice must be justified; that there is then production of knowledge must be justified. But the question of credentials isn't posed here concerning what is said about the practical state of problems and solutions. On repeated occasions problems and solutions are said to exist in the practical state but that statement, that certainty concerning what exists in the practical state is not subjected to any questioning as to right. So, one may wonder

3. V. I. Lenin, "What Is to Be Done?," in *Selected Works*, *1* (Moscow: Progress Publishers, 1977), 96.

4. Lenin, "What Is to Be Done?," 109.

5. Lenin, "What Is to Be Done?"

6. [Translator's Note]: A barely legible handwritten marginal insertion here—with a juxtaposed circled capital T—appears to read: "Read 2 times" [reference to page in Althusser, *For Marx*, concerning the context of this discussion; cf. 166–69].

7. Althusser, *For Marx*, 110.

what existing in the practical state, and in the practical state in the practice of Marxism—a notion that isn't explained here—means for problems and solutions. What is the place that is identified here by the name "practice of Marxism?" Althusser doesn't specify. Does it simply concern Marx's writing following the Break, and if so, on the basis of which indices can one recognize an existence of problems and solutions in the practical state within a text? What are the criteria for detecting that, what type of reading is presupposed, etc.? And if, as one can easily foresee, the "practice of Marxism" where that is found in the practical state is not only texts, these or those texts, these or those strata of Marx's text, well, the criteriology is even more difficult, it implies taking an active position, differentiated from all the phenomena that for more than a century it has been possible to classify under the rubric "practice of Marxism," where it is certain that the problems and solutions at the practical level weren't always to be found there, weren't always everywhere there, and weren't always equally so. In other words, "existing in the practical state in Marxist practice" functions here as a massive unproblematized premise of these protocols.

I now come to the definitions. They bear on two words and, if you wish, four concepts. The two words are Practice and Theory, the four concepts are practice in general, theoretical practice, theory, Theory.

Let's take a look at that.

1.[8] Practice in general: this is "any process of *transformation* of a determinate given raw material into a determinate *product*" (*For Marx*, 166).[9] Let us attend to every word and to the relation between each of the concepts that he names: transformation, process of transformation of a given raw material into a determinate product. Althusser underlines *transformation* and *product*. Transformation is a production. Practice is a productive transformation or a transformative production starting from a raw material. That transformation is said to be *effected* by a labor. The labor of transformation is defined as the decisive moment of the process; it is firmly predicated on practice in the strict sense, in the narrow sense according to Althusser. That strict sense is determined neither by the raw material nor by the finished product, but by the labor of transformation, by the *tra* if you wish (see above).

---

8. The numbering that begins here does not continue in the typescript. [Translator's note]: Subsequent numbering has been added for clarity below, in accordance with the four concepts Derrida has just listed.

9. [Translator's Note]: "Raw material" is *matière première* in French, literally "primary matter." Derrida's subsequent commentary draws on that sense of what is first or primary.

This labor of transformation is regularly defined as human; no practice that is not human. Humanity forms an indisputable part of this definition of practice. But not humanity alone: in the *tra* structure there are "men, means, and a technical method of utilizing the means" (167), but all that relates to the human. Not the human alone or human in the abstract: practice is always a social practice in a complex and structured socio-practical unity.

Two points are worth noting before proceeding: in this definition of the practical in the strict sense as labor of productive transformation, humanity, the human socius—granted, it is concrete—is an essential element, an essential predicate. What Althusser calls the "activity of living men" (ibid.), with all the problems posed by that formulation, belongs to the definition of the practical in general and in the strict sense. No critique of humanism, no question concerning the essential reference to the humanity of man, challenges or will come to challenge this implication of the human within the definition of praxis in general (announce Heidegger's questions). Second point: Althusser calls the link, within practice, between the "activity of living men," raw material and the means utilized, that of *technique*, more literally in this text "a technical method of utilizing the means" (167). Like the question of the human, the question of technique is therefore unavoidable in the field of this problematic. What is man? What is technique? What does labor mean, and production, and raw material? Those are questions whose response is enveloped within the definition of practice in general and in the strict sense.

In saying "enveloped" I am using a very enveloped expression that can be developed in two seemingly distinct ways, according to a distinction whose stakes I find to be absolutely decisive.

Enveloping can mean: This Marxist discourse presupposes an essence of humanity, of production as transformation of raw material, an essence of technique, etc., in short a network of philosophical determinations that have been handed down from the history of metaphysics; and in making practice a motif or value or essential reference, whose generality can no longer be exceeded, it makes of practice (thus of transformative production or human labor or human technique) the essential determination of being, of what is and what is to be thought. It does not say that what is essential is raw material, or the product, but, as Althusser reminds us, what is essential is the labor of transformation, the transformative production of human technique. From this point of view we can understand, in its principle in any case, what Heidegger says concerning Marxism and the perspective that he proposes to give to it, for example, in the "Letter on 'Humanism.'"

We'll of course come back to the Heideggerian problematic and to this text, which begins, let me recall, with these words: *Wir bedenken das Wesen des Handelns noch lange nicht entschieden genug*: "we are still far from pondering the essence of action decisively enough"[10] (*Handeln*: cf. Kant, the hand, etc.), which interprets the values of *theoria* and *praxis* as effects of the technical interpretation of thinking, based on an interpretation that Heidegger proposes here and elsewhere, of metaphysics as technical determination of the truth, of *alētheia* as *tekhnē*. Humanism is essential to that metaphysics, which belongs to the history of the truth of being: "Absolute metaphysics, with its Marxian and Nietzschean inversions, belongs to the history of the truth of being."[11] In this sense Marxism is also a humanist metaphysics founded on a technological determination of being as production. That is why, while recognizing that the Marxist concept of history is unique in modern times inasmuch as it allows one to recognize the essentiality of historicity in being itself (I'm simplifying), Heidegger specifies this, which I'll read directly from the text (once again in order to situate things in anticipation, for we'll come back to it later in a slightly more differentiated way): "But since neither Husserl nor—so far as I have seen till now—Sartre recognizes the essential importance of the historical in being [*die Wesentlichkeit des Geschichtlichen im Sein*], neither phenomenology nor existentialism enters that dimension within which a productive dialogue [*produktives Gespräch*] with Marxism first becomes possible."[12] In other words there is an essential grasp of the historiality of being in Marxism, and it is with Marxism more than with any other thinking of that era that one must understand clearly the truth of being. But once that is recognized, according to Heidegger—who thinks that wrenching Marxism out of a certain Hegelian determination of alienation and of labor is neither possible nor serious—one must stop thinking Marxism, and dialectical materialism as the simple affirmation of matter, or of a ground that is in the final analysis material, or of the idea that everything is in the final analysis only matter. Rather it should be thought on the basis of the essence of labor (or here, of transformation, of transformative labor, etc.). For example, he writes (read "Letter on 'Humanism'"):

---

10. Martin Heidegger, "Letter on 'Humanism,'" trans. Frank A. Capuzzi, in *Pathmarks*, ed. William McNeill (Cambridge: Cambridge University Press, 1998), 239; cf. "Brief über den Humanismus," in Heidegger's *Gesamtausgabe*, vol. 9, ed. F.-W. von Hermann (Frankfurt: Vittorio Klostermann GmbH, 1976), 145.

11. Heidegger, *Gesamtausgabe*, vol. 9, 256.

12. Heidegger, *Gesamtausgabe*, vol. 9, 259; see also 170.

For such dialogue it is certainly also necessary to free oneself from naive notions about materialism, as well as from the cheap refutations that are supposed to counter it. The essence of materialism does not consist in the assertion that everything is simply matter but rather in a metaphysical determination according to which every being appears as the material of labor. The modern metaphysical essence of labor is anticipated in Hegel's *Phenomenology of Spirit* as the self-establishing process of unconditioned production, which is the objectification of the actual through the human being, experienced as subjectivity. The essence of materialism is concealed in the essence of technology, about which much has been written but little has been thought.[13]

There you have one of the problematic directions in which one could develop what remains enveloped in what I was saying just now, when I said that the response to asking what work, production, matter, man, technique, etc., are,[14] is enveloped within the definition of practice in general and in the strict sense. The other direction—but is it absolutely other or discernable in the final analysis?—would consist in questioning whether Marxism doesn't precisely come to think for the first time what remained enveloped within the philosophemes production, technique, humanity, labor, etc., articulating together the possibilities of those philosophemes, which is to say accounting for metaphysics as a technological humanism rather than allowing itself to be comprehended by it, accounting for it no longer theoretically but by means of an essential, practical, etc. transformation.

I'll allow that question, that type of question to remain open; for now.

We are still restricting ourselves to the analysis of the first of the definitions proposed by Althusser. Social practice, which is implied in the definition of practice in general, is a complex unity including several distinct types of practice. Now, among those distinct practices that make up the structured unity of social practice there is one that constitutes it as final recourse, being "determinant in the last resort," namely "the practice of transformation of a given nature (raw material)" into *products*, into "useful *products* by the activity of living men working through the *methodically organized* employment

---

13. Heidegger, *Gesamtausgabe*, vol. 9, 259. [Translator's Note]: Derrida specifies pp. 103–4 of the French edition he is consulting: Heidegger, *Lettre sur l'humanisme*, trans. R. Munier (Paris: Aubier, 1964).

14. [Translator's Note]: This sentence ends here in Derrida's typescript. Cf. above p. 59, where the syntax seems to be resolved in the manner indicated: "Those are questions whose response is enveloped within the definition of practice in general and in the strict sense."

of determinate *means of production* within the framework of determinate relations of production" (*For Marx*, 167). In other words the essential element, determinant in the last resort, of practice as social practice is the transformation of nature as raw material into products; it is therefore production that starts out from natural raw material, production that starts out from nature, production as transformation of nature. The value of nature is not questioned here, it is simply opposed to the process that transforms it, here called transformation or transformative labor or production. Production is not natural, it is the transformation of nature by means of social practice. Such a production has all the characteristics of *tekhnē*, at least of the *tekhnē* that has come to be opposed to or distinguished from *physis* as reserve of raw material. But that opposition is in operation here, taken as read. Of course, it is not a matter of opposing nature in itself to an abstract production in itself. Althusser makes quite clear that this production is always determinate: "the *methodically organized* employment of determinate *means of production* within the framework of determinate relations of production." There is no general production but always determinate relations of production and means of production. Does that determination exempt one from referring to an understanding of production in general, to a concept of production in general? I hardly think so, especially because Althusser has just defined practice in general, which means in the end production in general, while recalling that practice is a complex structured and determinate unity. One must not confuse the concept X in general . . .[15] and the existence of an X in general.

What is production in general? How do all these definitions refer—as final recourse precisely, since the final recourse is the productive transformation of nature—how do they refer to the concrete essence of production, to the productive being-production of production, to the essence of technique as transformative production *of physis*, etc.? These are not abstract questions. Their stakes involve Marxism's relation to philosophy, the relation of Marxist philosophical specificity to the history of its concepts, to the history—philosophical or otherwise—of its concepts or philosophemes, etc. (Link with Heidegger? . . .)

Without persisting too much further in this vein at this point I'll underscore how, within the definition of practice in general, the concept of production operates on two different levels and in two different places, and not by chance. In the very paragraph involving that definition the concept

---

15. [Translator's Note]: This and the following ellipsis in typescript.

operates visibly, and the word itself is uttered, inscribed at the moment of determining practice as social practice in the last resort: the transformation of nature-raw material into products is indeed a *production*, production itself in the last resort; and, in the following sentence, the word is indeed uttered. But elsewhere, still in this paragraph, Althusser writes: "Over and above production social practice includes other essential levels: political practice . . . ideological practice . . . *theoretical practice*" (167). That doesn't mean that those three practices are not productive, that they aren't productions. Every practice is production (transformation of a raw material into products by human technique) but Althusser designates these three practices "over and above [*outre*] production," obviously implying that they are not production in the last resort, that is not the direct transformation of natural raw material. Simply put, though they are all productive, productive practices, these three levels (political, ideological, theoretical practice) are not productions at the level of the practice that determines in the last resort. The question raised here is therefore not only that of the concept of production (its qualifications, to repeat Althusser's legalistic vocabulary), but also that of the "last resort," elsewhere translated as "final recourse [*dernière instance*]."

Read *For Marx*, p. 167:

> Ideology is not always taken seriously as an existing practice: but to recognize this is the indispensable prior condition for any theory of ideology. The existence of a theoretical practice is taken seriously even more rarely: but this prior condition is indispensable to an understanding of what theory itself, and its relation to "social practice" are for Marxism.[16]

Then comes the second definition. It bears on one of the levels—I won't call them secondary, that would be inaccurate, but levels of the not-last, before-the-last resort. One of these levels of social practice. It concerns neither political practice nor ideological practice. Althusser doesn't define those here, he doesn't provide a definition properly speaking. It is theory or theoretical practice. It always implies, as we shall see, *something of the* ideological and *something of the* political, but it isn't political practice or ideological practice that Althusser declines to define here, since that isn't his topic.

<2.> What then is theory or theoretical practice? It is a *specific* form of social practice and it falls within the general definition of practice, that is to say it has all its characteristics: it works on raw material, raw material that

---

16. Cf. Althusser, *Pour Marx*, 168.

Althusser qualifies very quickly with three words in a parenthesis, a very rich parenthesis, therefore, but all the more problematic: "(representations, concepts, facts)" (167). The raw material (for some is also required) of last resort is here not nature but "representations, concepts, facts." This raw material is not therefore absolutely first, as nature is for production in the last resort, this first material of theoretical practice is already an informed, transformed product, and, Althusser says, it is "given" by other practices that he qualifies in this way: they are either *empirical*, *technical*, or *ideological*. Althusser does not expand on that any further. What is important here is that raw material, what functions as raw material for theoretical Practice[17] is already given by other practices, which makes it the product of other practices. In other words: production in the strict sense works at the level of nature (first first material); theoretical production works on second first material.

It is at this point that there is produced—within theory, then, as theoretical practice—a cleavage and an interesting displacement to which close attention must be paid. Theoretical practice in general can be scientific theoretical practice *or* prescientific theoretical practice. It is never a-scientific. It is always a relation to science, en route to or in view of science, in its very definition. The theoretical is defined by its relation to scientificity. So there is prescientific theoretical practice and scientific theoretical practice. Prescientific theoretical practice is ideological theoretical practice ("prescientific theoretical practice, that is, 'ideological,'" says Althusser [167]). The adjective "ideological" gives rise to a parenthesis intended to specify what is to be understood here by prescientific, that is to say ideological practice. What does one find in this parenthesis? "the forms of 'knowledge'"—with inverted commas around "knowledge" to indicate that these knowledges indeed have the form of knowledge but are not real true knowledges because they are prescientific—"the forms of 'knowledge' that make up the prehistory of a science and their 'philosophies'" (in the plural and in inverted commas) (ibid.). This situating of philosophy here matters to us a great deal. It signifies that prescientific theoretical, that is ideological practice, consisting of prescientific "knowledges" and belonging to the prehistory of a science have, can have, and even must always have had *their* philosophies, the philosophy or rather the philosoph*ies* corresponding to this ideological and prescientific state of theoretical practice. There would therefore be philosophies *corresponding to*—and one must indeed understand that here as *dependent on*—a prescientific and ideological state of theoretical practice. That

---

17. [Translator's Note]: Word capitalized in typescript.

doesn't mean that every philosophy, that philosophy in general depends on this ideological state, but that certain philosophies have done so. In other words, the epistemological break, which is going to appear immediately after in the definition, to draw the line between prescientific and scientific, will immediately have an effect on philosophy. It won't be said that there is prescientific philosophy and scientific philosophy but there will be forms of philosophy corresponding to prescientific theoretical practices and forms of philosophy corresponding to scientific theoretical practices.

<3.> Here is where one must situate the emergence within the definition of theoretical practice in general, and in that, within the definition of scientific theoretical practice, of something that Althusser then calls "theory," with a small "t." Theory with a small "t" will be the name for any scientific theoretical practice (beyond the epistemological break): "Restricting myself to the essential point as far as our analysis is concerned, I shall take up a position beyond the 'break', within the constituted science, and use the following nomenclature: I shall call *theory* any theoretical practice of a *scientific* character. I shall call 'theory' (in inverted commas) the determinate *theoretical system* of a real science (its basic concepts in their more or less contradictory unity at a given time)" (168).

Hence, small "t" theory is "any theoretical practice of a scientific character." So far so good. By always using the same word (theory in lowercase), but adding the graphic artifice of quotes in order to give to what is often called a theory its due—the theory of universal attraction, the theory of wave mechanics—Althusser proposes calling "theory" (lowercase in quotes) the determinate theoretical system of a real science, its "basic concepts in their more or less contradictory unity at a given time" (168). The "theory" of a science is the "reflection," within the complex and more or less problematic unity of its concepts, of its results now become conditions and means of its own theoretical practice. Among the examples of this type of "theory" Althusser names, following universal attraction and wave mechanics, then an "etc. . . . ," the "*theory*" (this time in italics, lowercase and quotes) of historical materialism. Historical materialism is thus a theoretical practice, a scientific theoretical practice, having broken with its ideological prehistory, and a scientific theoretical practice in the form of "theory." Since dialectical materialism, that is Marxist philosophy in its specificity, will have a privileged relation with historical materialism without being reduced to it, one must from here on anticipate that Marxist philosophy as dialectical materialism is a form of philosophy that is inseparable from a scientific theoretical practice having the form of a "theory" (small "t" and enclosed in quotes) (blackboard).

<4.> Well, this form of philosophy—the dialectical materialism inseparable from scientific theoretical practice in the form of "theory" (small "t" and quotes) that the historical materialism founded by Marx constitutes—this form of philosophy will be big "T" Theory. Theory (uppercase) will be the Theory of practice in general, "itself elaborated on the basis of the Theory of existing theoretical practices (sciences), which transforms into 'knowledges' (scientific truths) the ideological product of existing 'empirical' practices (the concrete activity of men). This Theory is the materialist *dialectic* which is one with dialectical materialism" (168).

What has happened in the course of these definitions? Althusser concludes by saying that they are required in order to give a "theoretically based" response to the problem of knowing what use there is in theoretically stating a solution existing in the practical state. The point was to fill the gap between theory and practice, but, in filling the gap, to produce forms of knowledge. What then has happened? Well, at least this (another dialectical circle recognized as indispensably necessary): that producing the definition of Theory, comes back, by the end of this definitional excursus, to the place out of which all of these definitions were produced or emitted, namely to the Theory (uppercase) of dialectical materialism. Indeed, if Theory (uppercase) is dialectical materialism, another name for Marxist philosophy in its specificity, it is also, and I am quoting, "the Theory of practice in general" (168), that is to say the Theory of all those definitions. It is defined and defining, the general condition of all those definitions and one defined object among all those definitions. In another form of the same circle, it is the theory of the break because it makes the break an essential criterion of the theoretical, of the distinction between scientific theoretical practice and prescientific theoretical practice. It is the theory of the break and an effect of the break, a delayed effect of the break [*un après-coup de la coupure*]. The theory of the epistemological break presupposes the break, with the result that if Theory as philosophy, as dialectical materialism, upon which all these definitions depend, if it isn't Science or the Science of Sciences (as it gives all the appearances of being), it is nevertheless indissociable from what is here called the epistemological break, dependent on it for its philosophical specificity, dependent on it also to the extent that, as theory of existing practices, it has a privileged link with "theory" as science, or with that science as "theory" called historical materialism. That is why in the Preface ("Today") it was said that the specific difference of Marxist philosophy depended on "an *epistemological break* . . . indicating the emergence of a new conception of philosophy" (32).

This positioning of theory/practice relations within a Marxist philosophy named Theory and starting from it, in that defining/defined circle, it is this philosophical positioning of Marxist philosophy as Theory that will be considered by Althusser to be a theoreticist deviation. In his "Reply to John Lewis" he reminds us that, in 1967, in the preface to the Italian edition of *Reading Capital*, he denounced that theoreticist deviation.

Read "Reply to John Lewis" (*Essays in Self-Criticism*, pp. 67–68) and comment:

> More precisely, I did not separate Marx's philosophical revolution from the "epistemological break", and I therefore talked about philosophy as if it were science, and quite logically wrote that in 1845 Marx made a *double* break, scientific *and* philosophical.
>
> That was a mistake. It is an example of *theoreticist* (rationalist-speculative) deviation which I denounced in the brief self-criticism contained in the Preface to the Italian edition of *Reading Capital* (1967), reproduced in the English edition. Very schematically, this mistake consists in thinking that philosophy is a *science*, and that, like every science, it has (1) an *object*; (2) a *beginning* (the "epistemological break" occurs at the moment when it *looms up* in the pre-scientific, ideological cultural universe); and (3) a *history* (comparable to the history of science). This theoreticist error found its clearest and purest expression in my formula: Philosophy is "Theory of theoretical practice."[18]

Next time we'll ask questions concerning the place, the new locus of philosophy (as condition of revolutionary science) in that self-critical trajectory. And asking questions concerning such a topics of the internal bordering [*bordure*] of philosophy on the basis of which the Theory/Practice pair gets invested, we'll begin to be interested by other displacements of this topics of the edge; others perhaps, perhaps others perhaps not; and we'll ask ourselves what is meant by a deviation from or rectification of the line between theoreticism and practicism, and whether there are (or are not), in that event, laws for "must be done."

---

18. Cf. Louis Althusser, *Réponse à John Lewis* (Paris: Maspero, 1973), 55–56.

FIFTH SESSION

Since we are running behind, and because other exposés will give us the opportunity to come back to it systematically, I won't develop our already embarked upon analysis of Althusser's trajectory beyond the moment when, for example in the Italian preface to *Reading Capital*, then in "Reply to John Lewis" and "Elements of Self-Criticism," he recognizes in the schema that we analyzed closely last time what in "Elements of Self-Criticism" he calls an "erroneous tendency" or deviation, namely theoreticism (*Essays in Self-Criticism*, 105); where he recognizes moreover that, and I quote, "the definition of philosophy as 'Theory of theoretical practice'" is "quite indefensible" (147) and represents "the highest point in the development of this theoreticist tendency" (124). Without entering into this movement of self-criticism or rectification, then, I will retain this point concerning our problematic, namely that the theory/practice pair, as endorsed by Marxist discourse, as alternatively inflected along a certain line (and we mused about what a line might be in philosophy and what problems that would raise or recast), inflected along a line that was here theoreticist there practicist, this pair belongs to something like philosophy, and there is a Marxist philosophy or a Marxist philosophical project, and it is from its inner edge that the theory/practice pair becomes a question. That doesn't mean, of course, that philosophy is sovereign or autonomous—and in fact it here represents, or translates forces and struggles that are not philosophical in and of themselves—but a Marxist philosophy, existing or to come, is what must determine the place and site of, and relations between theory and practice, which are in that sense philosophemes. The new definition that Althusser gives philosophy from "Lenin and Philosophy" on ("*intervention* in the theoretical domain," or, especially, in "Elements of Self-Criticism," "philosophy is, in the last instance, class struggle in theory"), this new definition is produced by and within a project of Marxist philosophy, and claimed as such. No doubt, this new definition is not that of a new philosophy, of a new philosophy of practice for example, but, as he writes at the end of "Lenin and Philosophy," "of a (new) practice of philosophy": "*Marxism is not a (new) philosophy of praxis* [Gramsci], *but a (new) practice of philosophy*" (68). Of course, everything is at stake within the parenthesis "(new)," in parentheses, for once the novelty is focused no longer on content but on practice, on the mode of practice, it may find itself either increased—it is no longer content that is renewed but practice, the way of doing, the doing that would transform even the essence of philosophy, but the essence of philosophy is still a philosopheme to be transformed—or decreased because the renewal of practice touches essentially neither on the content nor on the fact of this new practice's belonging to something like philosophy: it is a new practice of something that remains philosophy, identifiable as philosophy.

Read last paragraph of "Lenin and Philosophy":

> This new practice of philosophy can transform philosophy. And in addition it can to some extent *assist* in the transformation of the world. Assist only, for it is not theoreticians, scientists or philosophers, it is not "men" who make history—but the "masses", i.e. the classes allied in a single class struggle. (*Lenin and Philosophy*, 68)

The fact of all that taking place on the basis of a project of "Marxist philosophy" is something that the trajectory subsequent to its theoreticist moment will never belie, and that is what counts for us from the perspective in which we are situated. Not only is there, but there must be, there will be a Marxist philosophy, it must be done. And it is within the perspective of that project, of this philosophy already there but still to come, that Althusser writes: "the day is always long, but as luck would have it, it is already far advanced, look: dusk is now about to fall. Marxist philosophy will take wing" (*Lenin and Philosophy*, 43).

Naturally, from this inner edge of the philosophical, all philosophy, the entire definition of philosophy, the whole history of philosophy (and in it the history of the theory/practice pair) would be reinterpreted, notably on the basis of the intact, intangible framework proposed by Engels: the age-old struggle between two tendencies: idealism and materialism, Engel's "classical thesis" as Althusser calls it, to which Lenin gave "an unprecedented scope" (54).

What we'll hold on to for the moment, then, is the interpretation of the philosophical history of the theory/practice pair made from the inner edge of what, in a philosophical practice, is philosophical.

Naturally, the problematic I am proposing here by referring to the inner edge of the philosophical is not, as I see it, meant to produce demarcations, lines of demarcation or reassuring oppositions such as: here you have what is on this side, here you have what goes beyond, here is the limit, here the inner edge, here the outer edge, within vs. without. On the contrary, this problematic takes aim at the edge, it aims to problematize the security that a border provides, the trait that forms an edge. In the end the question would be less that of the inner or outer edge of the philosophical, of the inside or outside, on this side or over the other side, than the question "what is an edge?" why a border? What is the structure of something like an edge? And an edge, is it something? Is there any edge? etc.

The overflowing [*débordement*] of a philosophy by another, the overflowing of philosophy by a "thinking" that is no longer simply *philosophical*, such an overflowing is the essential trait (but how can an overflowing be a drawn line?) of every discourse (but is discourse theory or practice?) on the theory/practice relation. It is also the trait of discourse in general. If I take up again the statements I have just made (rereading them), I note, going back from the last to the first, in Marxist-Althusserian "discourse" for example, that what I identified as philosophical discourse on theory and practice would not lend itself to being so identified through and through. Although Althusser does not pose that type of question, he nevertheless makes it clear that at the moment when he identifies the Marxist project of a new practice of philosophy, at the moment when he defines the place of philosophy (as class struggle in theory), the defining discourse is no longer simply that of philosophy defining or situating itself; rather, this defining discourse is itself also an act, a political gesture, a practice, it is no longer a purely theoretical language, nor even an essentially theoretical practice. Theoretical and/or philosophical discourse, like discourse in general, overflows itself in the course of its operation. The Althusserian definition of the Marxist practice of philosophy intends to overflow not only all other philosophy, the whole history of philosophy thus able to be interpreted and transformed on the basis of sides taken in the class struggle; instead, it intends also to overflow the philosophical as such, once that is defined and even situated in a field (for example that of class struggle) that it doesn't control, and which is far from being reduced to its philosophical instance.

Philosophy overflowed [*débordée*], then. But overflowing, philosophy's overflowing itself, comprising itself and the rest, has always belonged to the philosophical. As a result the utterance proposing that the definition or situation of philosophy is not in itself philosophical is always difficult, unstable. Nothing is more philosophical that the act of defining or situating the philosophical within the general field of what is, of being as this or that, here production or practice.

Well then? Where to situate the edging across which philosophy overflows as it hems itself in, as it makes its bed? In the first of these utterances I have just reread there is this, the word "thinking": "the overflowing of philosophy by a 'thinking.'" Whatever one might explore as the semantic content of this word and reply to the question "what is called thinking"—something I leave to the side for the moment—the function of this word in my utterance was to mark a gap between philosophizing and thinking, as though there were in some way a *thinking* whose possibility and place were not simply philosophical, overflowing philosophy. Where am I trying to go with this thinking?

To Heidegger, you'll of course say, who distinguishes between philosophizing and thinking, and who in some way determines the limit of the philosophical on the basis of something like a thinking that would not yet, or would already no longer be simply philosophical. Heidegger then, but not so fast. I want to remain for a moment with Marxist-Althusserian discourse. On page 59 of "Lenin and Philosophy" a whole development takes to task, along classically Marxist lines, the idealism attached to interest in thinking as pure thought (apropos of Levi-Strauss). But on the previous page the word "thinking" is promoted in a quite unusual form for Marxist discourse. It is italicized and made the object of a positive evaluation whose orientation is very difficult to discern, whether toward thinking as conceptual-philosophical operation or a thinking that would already be more than philosophical. It is difficult to know whether, in the lines that I am going to read, "thinking" designates the philosophical rigor that conceptualizes what was not yet conceptualized, or what, in Lenin—for Lenin's thinking is what is in question—allows one to think the philosophical as such, on the basis of a thinking that is no longer simply philosophical:

Read "Lenin and Philosophy," p. 58: "Ultimately, though Engels has strokes of astonishing genius when he is working on Marx, his *thinking* is not comparable with Lenin's. It often happens that he juxtaposes theses—rather than *think* them in the unity of their relations."

Thinking designates in any case the overflow operation vis-à-vis the history of pre-Marxist philosophy. There is no doubt that—up to the present, and although to my knowledge there has never been any effective, rigorous, and to my mind satisfactory Marxist reading of Heidegger (or even of Nietzsche)—there is no doubt that beneath that non-reading lies the self-assured certainty that Heidegger is included in advance in the "age-old struggle" between idealism and materialism ("Lenin and Philosophy," 54), and that he represents a more or less subtle, original or overdetermined variant of the possibilities constituting that struggle. What is the value of that certainty? What reading is it dispensing with or protecting itself from? And when I ask from what reading it is protecting itself I am not appealing to a reading that would simply adhere to Heidegger but to a potentially deconstructive reading of him and of the questions he poses to Marxism, on the subject of Marxism and what he considers to be the meaning of Marxism.

For Heidegger undertakes an overflowing of Marxist discourse and its metaphysical space, and that counter-overflow is the place I wanted to get to.

All this takes place around the question of technique, which we have seen announced as an essential site, a schema, or schematism (in the analogously Kantian sense, if you wish) in the theory/practice opposition.

In the text "The Question Concerning Technology" (1953) no allusion is made to dialectical materialism. But in the "Letter on 'Humanism'" (1946) one can find *both* the essential schema situating technology as Heidegger sees it, which will be unfolded several years later in the lecture on technology, *and*, at the same time, then, a situating of Marxism in relation to the question of technique. I refer, then, in the case of this first situation, to the "Letter." I already laid down the basics when I quoted the sort of ambiguous homage that Heidegger pays to Marx there, to the Marx who recognizes historicity in the essentiality of being, and especially regarding modern materialism inasmuch as it isn't subject to refutation, inasmuch as it doesn't consist essentially in affirming that everything is only matter, but instead in "a metaphysical determination according to which every being appears as the material of labor [*Arbeit*]. The modern metaphysical essence of labor is anticipated [*vorgedacht*, thought in advance] in Hegel's *Phenomenology of Spirit* as the self-establishing process [*sich selbst einrichtender Vorgang*] of unconditioned production, which is the objectification of the actual [*Vergegenständlichung des Wirklichen*] through the human being, experienced as subjectivity."[1] What does that mean? And in what way is it, on one hand, able to define dialectical materialism and, on the other, able to refer to something like technique? Let's take these statements literally, word for word. It isn't untrue that for every dialectical materialism beings [*l'étant*] in general are determined in the last resort as matter, and as material of a labor and a praxis, matter referred to a praxis. That is precisely what, according to Marx himself, distinguishes his materialism from that of

---

1. Heidegger, "Letter on 'Humanism,'" 259. Cf. Heidegger, *Gesamtausgabe*, vol. 9, ed. F.-W. von Hermann (Frankfurt: Vittorio Klostermann, 1976), 340.

Feuerbach. Here, since Heidegger is talking here about the beings as material of a labor, that is to say a process of unconditioned production, that is to say as objectification of the real (effective) by the human as subjectivity, it is necessary once again—because here Heidegger's text is in literal conformity with the 1st thesis on Feuerbach—to quote this first thesis, which we have already commented on. What does Marx reproach Feuerbach for? Well, precisely for the latter's not having understood the relation of human activity as practice and as subjectivity: "The chief defect of all hitherto [comment: starting from the relation to praxis, everything will be reinterpreted] existing materialism [that of Feuerbach included] is that the thing [*Gegenstand*], reality [*Wirklichkeit*], sensuousness [*Sinnlichkeit*], is conceived only in the form of the *object* [Objekt] *or of contemplation* [Anschauung], but not as *sensuous human activity, practice*, not subjectively [*nicht subjektiv*]."[2] As I emphasized last time I read this passage with you, "subjective" here designates the relation of the object to the activity of the human subject, as praxis. And that is what Marx calls Feuerbach back to. That is why further along, without contradiction, Marx calls this activity objective (*gegenständliche Tätigkeit*). The activity of revolutionary practice-critique with which the thesis ends supposes that whole movement. That, then, is what Heidegger is recalling when he speaks of matter as material of a human labor, of a subjectivity. So, it will be said: but this is just the ambiguous text of the "Theses on Feuerbach." Heidegger is still referring, as one has often done, to a still "young" Marx; he isn't taking into account the break. But over and above all the variations of the break that we now know (Althusser's self-criticism in that regard), it is clear that on this point and on this theme no break, indeed no hypothesis even of a break has any sense or possibility. If you refer to Marx's draft introduction to his *Contribution to the Critique of Political Economy* (1857) you will see the fundamental role played there by the concept of production. And if there is no general production, Marx recalls, if production in general is only an abstraction, he makes clear that it is indispensable "to distinguish those definitions which apply to production in general, in order not to over-look the essential differences existing despite the unity that follows from the very fact that the subject, mankind, and the object, nature, are the same."[3] That is a fundamental thesis, which we must not lose sight of, and which upholds the whole discourse: every

---

2. Marx, "Theses on Feuerbach," 121.

3. Karl Marx, *A Contribution to the Critique of Political Economy*, trans. S. W. Ryazanskaya (New York: International Publishers, 1970), 190.

being, as matter, appears as a relation of *production* between a subject and an object, between a humanity and a nature that are fundamentally identical. The basis, then, is nature as production, the unity of the totality of being as production, whatever the subsequent differentiations or determinations of that production be. When Heidegger thus speaks of "the self-establishing process of unconditioned production" we can now understand why it is "self-establishing [*sich selbst einrichtend*]" and why "unconditioned."[4] Unconditioned and self-establishing itself precisely because this production is the final recourse, the ultimate determination of being [*être*] as nature put into operation by human praxis. Nothing conditions it and it therefore deploys and organizes itself. It is thus the ultimate determination of beings as beings, as they are and as they appear. That is why Heidegger says here that it is a metaphysical determination of what is, of what is in totality, that is to say nature—nature as the unity of which man forms a part according to Marx—a determination of beings as unconditioned production. And it is on this production (here *Herstellung*, elsewhere *Produktion*, etc.) that the question of technology will be brought to bear.

This determination is not one among others, nor is it a late arrival. Its modern specificity is a stage in a relay that leads, step by step, back through the whole history of metaphysics; within that history, according to Heidegger, technique is not a particular problem. The essence of dialectical materialism—and hence its concept of production—cannot be understood without reference to the essence of technique, the technique about which, says Heidegger, "much has been written but little has been thought."[5] For technique refers, and not only through its etymology, to the Greek *tekhnē* that Heidegger wants to bring out as nothing other than a mode of truth, a mode of rendering beings manifest, a type of *alētheuein*. That is Heidegger's, indeed, unusual and original gesture; to think *tekhnē* as *alētheia* or rather to bring out how the determination of *alētheia* (*physis*) in *tekhnē* is a fundamental event upon which the whole history of metaphysics depends:

> As a form of truth [*Gestalt der Wahrheit*] technology is grounded in the history of metaphysics, which is itself a distinctive and up to now the only surveyable [able to be encompassed by the gaze: comment] phase of the history of being. No matter which of the various positions one chooses to adopt toward the doctrines of communism and to their foundation, from the point of view of the history of being [*seinsgeschichtlich*] it is certain that

4. Heidegger, "Letter on 'Humanism,'" 259.
5. Heidegger, "Letter on 'Humanism.'"

an elemental experience of what is world-historical [*weltgeschichtlich*] speaks out in it. Whoever takes "communism" only as a "party" or a "Weltanschauung" is thinking too shallowly, just as those who by the term "Americanism" mean, and mean derogatorily, nothing more than a particular lifestyle.[6]

What then is the gesture that Heidegger proposes and that he here calls "thinking?" It is that of "freeing" us (*frei machen*) from this technical determination, from this "technical" interpretation of thinking that he traces back to Plato and Aristotle. It is within that technical determination—which coincides with metaphysics itself—that the opposition between *theōria* and *praxis* is produced. According to him, in fact, because since Plato and Aristotle the Greeks have thought thinking as *tekhnē*, because they have placed it in the service of *praxis* and *poiēsis*, of doing and making, of producing, we have arrived at the point—which is scarcely even paradoxical—of determining thought as theoreticist. In other words, from that point on the theoreticist is not opposed to the technical and, within it, to the practical; it is a mode of thinking as praxis. Thinking, taken in itself, Heidegger says (but what does "in itself" mean here?), is not praxis, but from the moment it is determined on the basis of the *praxical* demand we get to where, *reactively*, the essence of thinking comes to be determined as *theōria*. Reactively, Heidegger specifies, it refers to "a reactive attempt [*reaktiver Versuch*]"[7] to preserve the autonomy and properness of thinking (its *Eigenständigkeit*) over and against doing and acting, against praxis. But that theoreticist reactivity then depends totally, in its very possibility, on a first destination or determination of thinking as *praxis* or *poiēsis* and, therefore, *tekhnē*. As a result, the theoretical is not a specification of the practical and, more generally, of the technical. The traditional theoreticism of philosophy is an effect of its practicism and not its opposite; a specific effect of its initial practicism and hence of its technicism. In a seemingly slightly different sense, but one that is perhaps fundamentally analogous, Heidegger will here speak of theory as theoretical practice. The theoretical is privileged only within a space that privileges the *praxical* and technical dimension. Read "Letter on 'Humanism,'" p. 240:

> In order to learn how to experience the aforementioned essence of thinking purely, and that means at the same time to carry it through, we must free ourselves from the technical interpretation of thinking. The beginnings of that interpretation reach back to Plato and Aristotle. They take thinking

---

6. Heidegger, "Letter on 'Humanism'"; cf. *Gesamtausgabe*, vol. 9, 340–41. An ellipsis follows this quote in the typescript.
7. Heidegger, "Letter on 'Humanism,'" 240.

itself to be a τέχνη, a process of deliberation in service to doing and making. But here deliberation is already seen from the perspective of πρᾶξις and ποίησις. For this reason thinking, when taken for itself, is not "practical." The characterization of thinking as θεωρία and the determination of knowing as "theoretical" comportment occur already within the "technical" interpretation of thinking. Such characterization is a reactive attempt to rescue thinking and preserve its autonomy over against acting and doing.[8]

What then is this technique from which the practical and theoretical would basically be derivations and whose opposition consequently becomes secondary, however serious that opposition be. The interest of this attempt—whatever one think of its value or necessity—lies in its claiming to get back behind an opposition and understand the law of this opposition and this alternative, this interminable and inextricable debate, because the two terms in fact belong to the same nexus [*combinatoire*] within the same system. What then is technique?

Although it should indeed be done I cannot follow step by step the whole Heideggerian pathway through this question. I refer you in particular to the two first essays collected in *Essais et conférences* ("La question de la technique" and "Science et méditation [*Besinnung*]," 1953: they go together).[9] In the time available, and given our problematic, I'll have to be satisfied with pointing out a path for reading, interpreting and questioning these texts by Heidegger.

As a whole these essays perhaps constitute an attempt to think the unity of a history of metaphysics starting from its edge. For example, the history of metaphysics would be gathered within this determination of truth as technique, of *alētheuein* as *tekhnē*, a determination on whose basis the theory/practice pair is put in place and so allows itself to be positioned and derived, but in such a way that, contrary to appearances, the theoreticist dominance that can be identified in the history of philosophy does not come into opposition to a practicist dominance, no more than would theoreticist idealism be opposed to some practicist materialism, being instead the effect (no doubt reactively, but still the effect) of a *praxical* and in the first place technical project at philosophy's origin. So if that is indeed how things

---

8. Heidegger, "Letter on 'Humanism.'" [Translator's Note]: Derrida's typescript specifies pp. 31–33 in *Lettre sur l'humanisme* (this quote from 31).

9. Martin Heidegger, *Essais et conférences*, trans. André Préau (Paris: Gallimard, 1958). Cf. "The Question Concerning Technology," and "Science and Reflection" in *The Question Concerning Technology and Other Essays*, trans. William Lovitt (New York: Harper & Row, 1977). Further references to this volume included in text, identified as "Question" and "Science," respectively.

stand—beginning with the broadest brush—does Heidegger not presume, in a mode that would of course have to be specified, and which is certainly not that of a prejudice or error, but that would perhaps reproduce the presumption or assumption of philosophy, of the philosophical itself, namely that of the unity of its tradition and its element, its medium, doesn't Heidegger reproduce philosophy, philosophy's relation to itself at the very moment that he proposes to exceed [*déborder*] it, to think it, to think the philosophical from the vantage of its edge, to think the metaphysical as determination of *alētheuein* as *tekhnē*, a determination that would cover the whole theoretico-practical space and, for example, the modern and Marxist period of that determination? First question, first type of question.

Second question. In claiming to go back through thinking, if you wish, back behind metaphysics, behind techno-metaphysics, doesn't Heidegger reproduce this "reactive" search that would like to get back closer to the proper origin, and to save what is more initial, more proper, more originary, which the technical determination of truth has supposedly in some way set adrift, deporting, even threatening it. What at first sight legitimizes my two questions—they are moreover indissociable—is the fact that, clearly enough, Heidegger claims to think the modern conceptual and historical situation of technique and of the theory/practice pair by going back to the dawn of Greek antiquity, which presupposes a continuum of the tradition. Naturally, it isn't a philological or etymological return, nor, as he makes clear, a modern renaissance of antiquity, or an historical curiosity; it is rather a matter of becoming conscious of something that, having been thought or said (*das Gedachte und Gedichtete*) since the dawn of Greek antiquity, in poetic form for example, "is still present today, present [*gegenwärtig*] in such a way that its essence [*Wesen*], which is still hidden from itself, everywhere comes to encounter us and approaches us most of all where we least expect it, namely, in the rule of modern technology [*Herrschaft der modernen Technik*], which is thoroughly foreign to the ancient world, yet nevertheless has in the latter its essential origin [*Wesensherkunft*]" ("Science," 158).[10] The return to this essential origin is therefore possible and must traverse a no doubt very differentiated element, but one whose differences don't affect its fundamental unity. Another legitimation, at first glance, for my questions: reactivity back toward the most original, the project of *saving* what is proper to the beginning, and on that side of techno-metaphysics is clearly formulated.

10. Cf. Heidegger, "Wissenschaft und Besinnung," *Gesamtausgabe*, vol. 7, ed. F.-W. von Hermann (Frankfurt: Vittorio Klostermann, 2000), 41. Where appropriate, page references to "Wissenschaft und Besinnung" will henceforth follow the English reference in text, preceded by the abbreviation *G7*.

Of course, it doesn't present itself as reactive, on the contrary it aims to erase a reactive theoreticism that reacts to an essential practicism of philosophy. Nevertheless, one may wonder whether that gesture doesn't reproduce, once more, the very schema that it seeks to contradict. One clue or point of reference: toward the end of "The Question Concerning Technology" it is said that even if technique is not in itself threatening, the essence of technique does represent the essential danger, and that such a threat has affected man in his being. And that threat is "the possibility that it could be denied to [man] to enter into a more original revealing [*ursprünglicheres Entbergen*] and hence to experience the call of a more primal truth [*den Zuspruch einer anfänglicheren Wahrheit zu erfahren*]" ("Question," 28).[11] Of course, where there is danger—and Heidegger here quotes Hölderlin, "grows the saving power also [*wächst das Rettende auch*]" (ibid.)—but it is indeed a matter of saving by returning to the most initial and most originary call. What difference can there be between what is called elsewhere, concerning theoreticism, a "reactive attempt," and this salvation, this safe conduct toward the origin; in what way would this "safe" be affirmative, that question remains.

The questions that I have just sketched out are simple and preliminary. However I wouldn't want them to be too simple, simplified or simplistic. Before measuring them against Heidegger's text, the force and richness of a text that, in any case, such questions, however legitimate, could not reduce or impoverish—nor could they limit it to all sorts of current schemas, and which, anyway, it already understands in a powerful way—before measuring these questions against the text, I'll outline two general precautions.

The first concerns the unity of the philosophical tradition and of the medium through which Heidegger wants to lead us back behind techno-metaphysics. That unity is not a simple, repetitive and undifferentiated homogeneity for Heidegger; he recognizes essential displacements within it, even irreducible mutations, for example that of Latin conceptuality or of modern technique, which configure a new space. But those displacements aren't absolute; they aren't ruptures or radical heterogeneities, and in order to think them as in fact displacements one has to go back to the essential origin and to the unity of the element, of the historial medium.

The second precaution concerns the threatening and the safe. For Heidegger it isn't about reacting against technique in the sense of what is often

---

11. Cf. Heidegger, "Die Frage nach der Technik," *Gesamtausgabe*, vol. 7, ed. F.-W. von Hermann (Frankfurt: Vittorio Klostermann, 2000), 29. Where appropriate, page references to "Die Frage nach der Technik" will henceforth follow the English reference in text, preceded by the abbreviation *G*7.

identified as a reactionary and naturalist, even ecologist ideology. Heidegger often insists on that: technique isn't "the work of the devil" ("Question," 26), nor is it a question of going back before technique, whether ancient or modern. Nevertheless, if technique isn't threatening, the essence of technique—which is not itself technique (see beginning of essay, comment)—is danger. That obviously avoids reaction, a reactivity against technique in its current ideological schema, but it can also aggravate, radicalize, essentialize it, and give to it its weight as thinking, its *pesant pensant*.[12]

Having taken these two precautions, let us try to proceed in such a way that, in reading Heidegger as in reading any other text, our critical vigilance does not hide from us the importance and necessity of what his text produces.

Since I won't have time today to pursue further the reading of these two texts—and I will in any case limit myself to something schematic—instead of taking up that reading I am going to make a brief detour by way of Aristotle. It happens that reference to Aristotle plays a major role in these two texts: once concerning the question of technique in the context of causality and his four causes; again, closer still to our problematic, in *"Wissenschaft und Besinnung"* concerning the difference between *theōria* and *praxis*, *bios praktikos* and *bios theōrētikos*. I'll start out from this second reference that is as close as can be to our problem.

Having begun with the common statement that "Science is the theory of the real [*Die Wissenschaft ist die Theorie des Wirklichen*]" ("Science," 157 [G7, 40]), he arrives at a point where he asks what "theory" means, the word "theory." He recalls that it comes from the verb *theōrein*, formed from *thea* and *horaō*. *Thēa*, as in theatre, means aspect, visible appearance, the aspect that Plato calls *eidos*. "To have seen this aspect, *eidenai*, is to know" (163). The second component is *horaō*, to look at, to consider in the light. The mode of life allied with *theōrein* is called by the Greeks *bios theōrētikos*. The *bios praktikos* is instead allied with acting (*Handeln*) and producing (*Herstellen*). Nevertheless, it must not be forgotten that *bios theōrētikos* is also conceived of as an activity, and the highest, most accomplished form of human existence. *Theōrein* relates to what is seen (through the sensible or intellectual eye—comment), to the aspect of the thing that is present, aspects important to man (important: value, honor, dignity, involvement, affairs; practice, etc.), aspects that *concern* man by means of their appearing (*scheinen*), and in which the presence of the Gods shines (phenomenon, *Schein*). What is

---

12. [Translator's Note]: *Peser*, to weigh, and *penser*, to think, share an overlapping etymology.

more, *theōrein* is what allows the *archai* and *aitiai* of things present to be perceived and exposed. It is at this point that Heidegger—while noting that he can't go into that topic here for it would require us to understand what the Greeks understood by those words, which we have for a long time interpreted as *principium* and *causa*, principle, ground and cause—refers in parentheses to a text of Aristotle's that he doesn't comment on, and which I'd like to look at with you. It is the *Nicomachean Ethics*, Bk. VI, chap. 2, 1139ff (cf. "Science," 163–64, [G7, 46]).

Aristotle has just divided the virtues of the soul (*tes psychēs aretas*) into two types: those of character (*ethos*) and those of the intellect (*dianoia*). And since he has dealt with ethical virtues in detail he now undertakes to explicate the others (dianoetic). He recalls that, among those, he had also distinguished two parts of the soul, *logon echon* (which has reason) and *alogon* (irrational). Pursuing that division, he distinguishes, within *logon echon*, two parts: that is where the theoretical and practical appear (inside the *logos*, then). One of the rational parts of the soul allows us to look at [*theoroumen*: the translation says "contemplate"—see Heidegger's commentary] "the kind of things whose principles [*archai*] cannot be other than they are" [very important for how the theoretical is constantly defined: can't intervene in or change what it looks at for it is dealing with what cannot be otherwise—comment, cf. Hegel's theoretical and practical senses].[13] The other part of the soul as *logon echon* is the part that knows contingent things, which can be other than they are, and since there is an affinity between what knows and what is known, there is a rational part of the soul that is made for knowledge of the contingent. Aristotle calls that part *logistikon* (logistical, calculating, deliberative), for one can calculate and deliberate on only contingent things, things that can be otherwise (different from Plato who places the *logistikon* at the summit of the three parts of the soul), and he calls epistemic, scientific, *epistemonikon*, the theoretical part dealing with the necessary and immutable, which cannot therefore change what is inasmuch as it doesn't change. So, as Aristotle there insists, the logistical, calculating part is simply one part of the soul that has the *logos*. What must be understood, though, is that each of the parts has what is best (*hexis*: aptitude), and hence its virtue, the virtue relating to its proper work, to what it does that is proper to it (*pros to ergon to oikeion*).

---

13. Cf. Aristotle, *Nicomachean Ethics*, trans. W. D. Ross, in *The Basic Works of Aristotle*, ed. Richard McKeon (New York: Random House, 1941): "We contemplate the kind of things whose originative causes are invariable" (1023).

There are three things proper (*kuria*) to *praxis* and to *alētheia* in the soul: *aesthesis*, *nous*, *orexis*: sensation, intellect, desire. *Aisthesis* does not instigate any praxis (cf. animals; *praxis*: human). Within the order of *dianoia*, or *nous*, the broadest object of this exposition by Aristotle—which is therefore what interests us here—affirmation and negation have correspondences on the side of desire, of *orexis*, in research (*dioxis*) and flight (*phugē*). Consequently, since ethical virtue is a *hexis* capable of choice (*proaieresis*), and since choice is a deliberative desire (*orexis bouleutikē*), there must, through a sort of collaboration between *nous* and *orexis*, be *logon alēthen* (rule or correct *logos*) and right desire (*orexis orthen*): identity between affirmed *logos* and pursued or pursuing desire. Now this thinking and truth (*dianoia*, *alētheia*) are in this case of the *practical* order (because there is desire, etc.). As for theoretical thinking (*thēoretikē dianoia*), which is neither practical nor poetic, it is regulated by the true and false only, contrary to practical intellect, which indeed also deals with truth (and is indeed also an intellect, reason) but with a truth of desire, of right or correct desire, of *orthodesiring*.

Before going further, I want to insist on the fact that the opposition between practical and theoretical is here internal to reason, to *logos* and *dianoia*. There is a practical reason and a theoretical reason. The fact that a hierarchy places the theoretical above the practical does not make the practical something foreign to rationality. Roots of Kantianism, etc. The same goes for desire (cf. *Critique of Judgment*: practice and desire, right desire). And this theoretico-practical structure of the *logos* is essentially anthropological. It is man: desire + reason. Within that system neither the theoretical and practical, nor theoretico-practical reason, can be defined without remaining inside a certain anthropologism, which Heidegger would call a metaphysics as humanism. And in fact Aristotle writes a little further along: "*dio ē oretikos nous e proairesis ē orexis dianoetikē, kai ē toiautē archē anthropos*: thus [one could just as well say "either"] proairesis (preferential choice, preference) is a desiring *nous* (*orektikos nous*) or a dianoetic desire (intellectual desire: *orexis dianoetikē*), and that principle is man."[14]

---

14. "Hence choice is either desiderative reason or ratiocinative desire, and such an origin of action is a man" (Aristotle, *Nicomachean Ethics*, 1024). [Translator's Note]: Barely legible handwritten notes at the end of this session appear to read: "1) Overflowing = transgression of the line; → logos-praktikos <illegible>—desire (transgression—transformation)—man. Must be done.
2) Heid<egger>

SIXTH SESSION

We are over the edge.[1] Whence our fatigue.

We are truly over the edge.

Truly. Truly, which doesn't qualify the way in which we would be over the edge, truly over the edge, because to tell the truth perhaps we are not at all over the edge, in truth. "Truly" means rather that if there is going over the edge [*débordement*], if there is an overflowing effect, it is an effect of truth. It is in the name of truth that it always overflows.

Last time, at a stage of our trajectory that I won't resituate, when we deemed it necessary to again pose the question of the edge, of the structure of the edge, we indeed saw that the overflowing of discourse, the overflowing of one philosophy by another, of philosophy by thinking, we indeed saw that that overflowing was always happening in truth, in the name of truth. It is not only in the name of truth that a philosophical project claims to flow over another, it is also in the name of truth that one claims to overflow the philosophical in general with, or in the direction of thinking. Remember what we were reading from Heidegger last week. It was in the name of a more initial, more originary truth, one not yet occupied or determined by *tekhnē*, by the techno-logical interpretation of *alētheuein*, it was in the name of that pre-philosophical, pre-metaphysical, pre-technological truth that he called for thinking, for thinking on this side of or beyond a theory/practice pair that allegedly wholly belongs to that techno-metaphysical regime of truth. Truth overflows a truth about truth, truth overflows, in thinking, a determined truth of truth.

Is truth therefore edgeless?

Note carefully that the "it must be done [*il faut le faire*]" that opened this seminar was itself an excessive [*débordant*] gesture, not a gesture describing or declaring some excess, but as much an excessive gesture as a formulation

---

1. [Translator's Note]: *débordés*, overworked, overwhelmed (overflowed).

of the excessive gesture. You remember that we decided to analyze the "doing" (praxis) in "it must be done," but also that we recognized that *must* was inscribed in every "doing"; and what's more, that *faut le faire* was a response to some sort of "transgression": what cheek, they dared to, etc., they stepped over the line, overstepped the bounds. *Ah, faut le faire*. It went over the top. The relation of doing or praxis to the law begins to come into focus. And we can now understand better how the political or moral question (the question of pure practical reason) cannot be dissociated from it, thanks to the detour we made through Kant (we'll come back to that), and the turn that led us to the *Nicomachean Ethics* at the end of last week's session. There we discovered:

1. that the *praxical* was indeed one of the two possibilities of logos, and even of the soul as *logon echon*. No praxis can be defined, nor has it ever been defined outside the system of this *logos* and of what has *logos*. As a result the theory/practice opposition is from that point of view indeed very dependent and derivative.
2. that the *praxical* presupposes *orexis*, desire, and an intellectual desire (marked not only by *logos* but by dianoetic intellectuality: dianoetic desire or desiring dianoia [*oretikos nous/orexis dianoetikē*], says Aristotle, it's one and the same). The relation of praxis to desire and to the law is thus posed as essential. A being without desire, without *logos*, and without law has no practical behavior or *hexis* (aptitude). Praxis is thus also a relation to the edge or to the limit.
3. we have seen that praxis was reserved for the being called man, man as being *logon echon* and made of a mixture of desire and dianoia, in opposition to the animal that, having only *aisthesis*, cannot deliberate and so accede to praxis. We are here provided with the continuous thread that, all the way up to and including Marx, reserves praxis for man, and withholds it, along with labor, from the animal. In *Capital* (Vol. I, Part III, Ch. VII), as you know, he writes: "We pre-suppose labour in a form that stamps it as exclusively human." And to justify that anthropologistic restriction Marx indeed refers to *logos*, to *dianoia*, to deliberation (*orexis bouleutikē*), in continuing: "We presuppose labour in a form that stamps it as exclusively human. A spider conducts operations that resemble those of a weaver, and a bee puts to shame many an architect in the construction of her cells. But what distinguishes the worst architect from the best of bees is this, that the architect raises his structure in imagination before he erects it in reality. At the end of every labour-process, we get a result that already existed in the imagination of the labourer at its

commencement. He not only effects a change of form in the material on which he works, but he also realises a purpose of his own that gives the law to his modus operandi, and to which he must subordinate his will."[2]

This anthropological space of the concepts of labor and praxis is therefore quite clear, and if, as Heidegger says, every metaphysics is fundamentally humanist, then so, to that extent, is the theory/practice opposition, notwithstanding for the moment whatever questions we might have asked last time about Heidegger's line of thinking, and whatever response they called for.

We were led to the reference to Aristotle by an undeveloped remark by Heidegger ("we can't go into this subject here"[3]) in *"Wissenschaft und Besinnung"* ("Science and Reflection"). I come back to that now. Why does this text interest us? In the first place because it concerns *theōria* and *praxis*, of course. But less obviously because of two motifs that I'll begin by situating: 1. Mark; 2. Edge.[4]

1. Mark: *Besinnung*, which is very inadequately translated into French as "meditation," here occupies a place that would be distinct *both* from science, of course (*Wissenschaft und Besinnung*), *and* from philosophy or technological metaphysics. It is about getting beyond, or back behind philosophy as metaphysics and/or science. *Besinnung* is here on the side of thinking qua overflowing of the philosophical. But, more specifically, Heidegger isn't content to use a word that is after all quite common in German, quite frequently translated as meditation, reflection, realization [*prise de conscience*] (cf. Husserl). He explains his choice of word and justifies it by as it were reconstituting its scope through reference to an etymology that is more important here for what he *does with* it, precisely, the way he works and practices it, than for what it is. The German etymology refers the *sinnen* of *besinnen* to *sinnan* (Old High German), for *Sind-nan*, which would be derived from *Sind*, path, step [*marche*]. What is noteworthy [*remarquable*], and especially marked, over-remarked in this seemingly etymological operation is: A. that it follows a trajectory, a path, a crossing through language toward a hidden sense (*Sinn* is also the word for that), a crossing that goes in the

---

2. Karl Marx, *Capital*, Vol. 1, ed. Frederick Engels (London: Lawrence and Wishart, 1967), 174.

3. Cf. "Science," 164: "The further characterization of *theōrein* ... cannot be given here; for this would require a reflection on what Greek experience understood in that which we for so long have represented as principium and causa, ground and cause (See Aristotle, *Nicomachean Ethics*, Bk. VI, chap. 2, 1139ff)."

4. [Translator's Note]: The numbered words are a handwritten addition. "1. Mark" again appears in the margin next to the following paragraph.

direction [*sens*] of sense, that walks [*marche*] in the sense of sense, hence of a step [*marche*] that marches in the sense of marching, which signifies that it works [*marche*] in the sense in which it marches and that there is therefore no sense to walking other than the step. No sense in *la marche*, no prior or subsequent direction or teleological edging for *la marche* that is not *la marche* itself. It walks/works the way it walks/works, or in order for it to walk/work, and that is what is especially marked here, if, as I have marked elsewhere, *marche* and *marque* intersect.

What is noteworthy also is: B. that this step that claims to come back or go over behind the theory/practice pair, toward a place where the technological and metaphysico-technological covering over that puts in place the theory/practice opposition hasn't yet taken place, this step (or this *Besinnung*: meditation) is already a praxis: not only because it goes to work on language and isn't a theory but also because, as we saw to begin, *prattein* always carries the value of a traversal, TRA (transformation, translation, tra),[5] a displacement that crosses over, a step. Of course, that is not by chance and that is why I am dwelling on it. You can be sure that each time you try to cross over the edge of [*déborder*] the opposition theory/practice you'll be doing it with a gesture that will sometimes be analogous to a practice, sometimes to a theory, sometimes to both at once. That irreducible analogy is what impels me to pose the question of the edge: each time there is overflow it resembles what is overflowed, overflowing remains in *affinity* with what is overflowed, *affined* and I'll even say confined to what is overflowed. Sometimes, I was saying, it is analogous to one of the terms of the pair (for example to praxis), sometimes to the other, sometimes to both. That is the case here: *Besinnung* is at the same time a journey, a *praxical* crossing back behind praxis, but also a passive praxis that lets be or be done and in that way resembles theory. It bears within it the pair on that side of whose birth it leads back to, or with which, if you wish, it is pregnant. It repeats the pair that it must account for, and all the way to the dialectic that will render them indissociable. To make you more aware of that I'll read, or rather retranslate (TRAnslation) in this way: "new questions would have to be asked [*neue Fragen*]. However, once we are aware of the latent [unapparent] situation in a direction [*Wegrichtung*] [a sense of a path, orientation along a path, via a way (*une voie*)] that brings us toward *das Fragwürdige*, what is worthy of questioning. In distinction to what is simply in doubt [*fraglich*] and everything that is without question [*fraglos*], the *Fragwürdiges* accords [*verleiht*] a clear incitation [*Anlaß*] and free support [*Anhalt*: *Anlaß* then

---

5. The parenthesis is the presumed reading of an interlinear handwritten addition.

Anhalt], thanks to which we can respond to what is said to [corresponds to] our being [*unser Wesen*] and calls it toward us. The voyage [*Wanderschaft*] in the direction [way: *Wegrichtung*] of the *Fragwürdiges* is not an adventure [*Abenteuer*] but a *Heimkehr* [return to one's birthplace, says the *tra*, a return to being "at home,"[6] chez soi, in one's *Heimat, Heimlichkeit*]."[7] It is indeed then a return path, but as Heidegger often says the path is what counts more, constitutes what is essential in it, counts more than the endpoint, the endpoint moreover being here a difference, the thinking of a difference. I continue my translation: "To set out along a *Wegrichtung*, along a path that a thing [*Sache*: proceeding, business, litigation] has already taken, that is called in our language *sinnan, sinnen*. *Sich auf den Sinn einlassen* [get involved in, enter into the *Sinn*, sense] *ist das Wesen der Besinnung*, such is the essence of *Besinnung*. That means more than the simple realization [*prise de conscience*] [*Bewußtmachen*: that is how *Besinnung* often gets translated] of something. We are not yet close to [haven't arrived at] *Besinnung* when we are no further along than consciousness. *Besinnung* is more [hence a certain practice of traversing, a certain march or mark, a certain sending-on-the-way (*en-voie*); more than consciousness—comment]." And this is where this praxis [*praxique*] of sending-on-the-way now starts to look like *theōria*, in that such a praxis, the pacing [*pas*] of praxis, this not-praxis is also a passive pacing. "*Besinnung* is more. It is *Gelassenheit* [calm, abandon, serenity, openness that lets be], abandon to the *Fragwürdiges*." So where does this passive pacing lead us, a pacing whose stepping practice is not yet the practice of philosophy, and whose passivity is not yet theory or the theoretical activity of philosophy, which, however, also lets be? It leads us where we already are and have been for a long time. Continuing: "Through *Besinnung* understood in this way we properly [*eigens*] arrive where, without having experience [*Erfahren*: also a relation to voyaging, to the ordeal of traversing] of it and without seeing it all the way through [*durchschauen*], we have been sojourning [holding ourselves up] for a long time. In *Besinnung* we go toward a place [*Ort—Erörterung*, etc., comment], and starting from there

6. [Translator's Note]: In English in the original.
7. Cf. "Science," 179–80 (*G7*, 63): ". . . would require that we pose further questions. Through this pointing to the inconspicuous state of affairs we are, however, directed onto a way that brings us before that which is worthy of questioning. In contradistinction to all that is merely questionable, as well as to everything that is 'without question,' that which is worthy of questioning alone affords, from out of itself, the clear impetus and untrammeled pause through which we are able to call toward us and call near that which addresses itself to our essence. Traveling in the direction that is a way toward that which is worthy of questioning is not adventure but homecoming."

space [*Raum*] simply opens that each time is traversed by [again the crossing motif—practice, *durchmisst*] our *Tun und Lassen*."[8] [Comment]

2. The second of these two motifs, the second preliminary heading of interest to us in this text concerns the EDGE. Actually, it doesn't concern the edge, it is itself concerned, provoked and invested, delimited by something that isn't the edge and isn't some thing, and that Heidegger calls the inescapable [*incontournable*], more rigorously *das Unumgängliche*.

The non-thematizable theme of what can't be gotten around can't be gotten around in this text. The word "inescapable [*unumgänglich*]" includes at least two meanings: A. it indeed is a matter of stepping or proceeding, what goes or comes on the path, *Gang*; B. it concerns what stepping can't get around, hence what it can neither avoid, circumvent, bypass—being always already enveloped, included in it—nor enclose totally as a totality that is comprehensible, limitable, surroundable [*bordable*] (edges without edge).

How is this inescapable announced? The text is called "*Wissenschaft und Besinnung*." *Besinnung* is on the path to what for science is unsurroundable, what science can't *determine*, what science as theory [theory of the real: "Science is the theory of the real"—*die Theorie des Wirklichen*, founding definition], what science as theory can't determine, whose term, limits, contours it can't recognize, quite simply because that forms the very conditions—one could almost say, but no . . .[9]—the transcendental conditions of possibility of the theoretical and of the scientific itself. The inescapable, inaccessible to theory and science, this inaccessible inescapable [*unzugängliches Unumgängliches*] (cf. "Science," 177 [*G7*, 61]), which is therefore both inevitable and impossible to define, for science is always announced according to the same schema, a transcendental ontological schema even if it does not take on the form of the classic transcendental (Kant,[10] Husserl).

---

8. Cf. "Science," 180 (*G7*, 63): "To follow a direction that is the way that something has, of itself, already taken is called, in our language, *sinnan, sinnen* [to sense]. To venture after sense or meaning [*Sinn*] is the essence of reflecting [*Besinnen*]. This means more than a mere making conscious of something. We do not yet have reflection when we have only consciousness. Reflection is more. It is calm, self-possessed surrender to that which is worthy of questioning.

Through reflection so understood we actually arrive at the place where, without having experienced it and without having seen penetratingly into it, we have long been sojourning. In reflection we gain access to a place from out of which there first opens the space traversed at any given time by all our doing and leaving undone."

9. [Translator's Note]: Ellipsis in typescript.

10. [Translator's Note]: The initials "M. A." appear before "Kant," perhaps referring to Marx and Althusser.

That is to say, science cannot make an object of what is its element, condition of possibility or even its essence. One of the traits of modern science as theory of the real is the delimitation of regions, domains of objects, specializations. Now in each of these regions the determinate science is, as such, incapable of thinking (gaining access to, circumnavigating) what it presupposes. Heidegger gives four examples: physics can't gain access to what is inescapable in it, namely *physis*, the objectivity of nature to which it relates being but one of the manners by which *physis* is determined. Science (theory) cannot even, as such, go into that question. In the same way, for psychiatry—a further example to be developed—human *Dasein* remains inescapable: "Dasein, in which man as man ek-sists, remains that which for psychiatry is not to be gotten around" ("Science," 175). Similarly, for history as science (*Historie*), history (*Geschichte*) remains as something that can't be gotten around; and the same for philology, linguistics, the science of writings, stylistics, poetics, etc., language remains what can't be gotten around. These four examples or figures of what can't be gotten around (*physis*, *Dasein*, *Geschichte*, *Sprache*), are not four dissociable examples, and as they are all inescapable they neither limit nor circumscribe themselves. They are the same inescapable (*physis*, *Dasein*, *Geschichte*, *Sprache*: tongue, language), inaccessible to science or theory as such, condition of theoretical determination but, by the same token, themselves inaccessible to that determination. And it is toward what is inescapable in the theoretical that *Besinnung* is in tra-jectory toward thinking.

There then, very schematically put, you have the two motifs (mark and edge) that I wanted to begin by recognizing in the essay *"Wissenschaft und Besinnung."*

I come back now to the point in the text where the necessity of the inescapable is announced.

One has indeed to see how history intervenes in this meditation, in its forward march [*dans cette marche*]. It doesn't deal, as though there had been no historical mutation, with a timeless structure called "science or theory" and whose impassive continuum could be grasped simply by finding its origin. There is a modern science, a modern technique, and in it something new, something structurally and essentially new, is taking place, even if one has to go back further to understand what that newness is.

What is happening that is new? Something new is happening that precisely has to do with the edge. The relation to the inescapable is being modified because something in modern science or theory is in some way being regionalized. Science is traversed by interior limits, it defines fields of objectivity, districts, circumscriptions, domains, framings, and specialized theory as something framed is all the less capable of gaining access to an inescapable that nevertheless renders it possible and activates it. According to Heidegger it is all the less capable of thinking the totality of beings (*physis*) from which it shapes its object or the domain of its object, less capable of thinking its history, language, and ek-sistence that constitute its element. Now, Heidegger has proposed a path [*trajet*] for grasping once again, through "thinking," this theoretico-scientific modernity. That path tends precisely to bring out a certain discontinuity, namely that if modern science is or appears as "theory," theory is there something essentially different from the Greek *theōria*. What is that otherness? That otherness—and this is not the least paradox here—is that modern theory is no longer a contemplation, or a passive or disinterested vision, but an active, intervening elaboration, as if going against its essence. It is in a certain way practical, practico-technical, and that makes for a disturbing *Unheimlichkeit* (Heidegger's word) that should give thinking pause. In what way is modern theory an elaboration (labor, therefore, and almost persecutory intervention: the motif of persecution seems to me to be present in Heidegger's text, I'll show that in more detail in a moment, even if it isn't present by name or in person)? In what way is modern theory an elaboration? Well, for that we are going to have to follow the text closely, in its most demanding word for word sense.

Let's take it up again from the beginning.

Heidegger starts out from the notion of *Kultur*. Although culture often designates the set of human spiritual and creative activities, although art and science are sometimes included in it also, neither art nor science can be reduced to cultural activity. Science—limiting ourselves to that—is not simply one of the modes of culture. Western European science is something that determines, in its fundamental traits, the reality in which the human stands today, and it is not the effect of a simple human willing that then fabricates it, makes it and dominates it, no more than it is the effect of what is naively believed to be understood by the name of a simple will to know (*ein bloßes Wissenwollen*). This "will to know" is itself activated by something else, by another (*ein Anderes*) that exerts its power over it (*waltet*) and conceals itself in our everyday representations of science. Science reigns everywhere, in industry, economic activity, education, politics, military strategy. In what, then, consists the essence, the being of this science that thus reigns everywhere, and the other that is concealed in its representation? Heidegger proposes an everyday formula: *Die Wissenschaft ist die Theorie des Wirklichen*, which we would translate as "science is the theory of the real" were it not for the fact that the word "real" fails to convey what is essential, namely the reference that the word *Wirkliches* makes to *wirken*, that is to an operation, labor, elaboration, in other words an effectivity supposing some efficiency, as will indeed be seen . . .[11] The formula "science is the theory of the effective" is, if you like, what Heidegger presents not as a solution or response, but on the contrary as a set of questions. It aims at modern science and is not the case for the science of the middle ages or of antiquity. Medieval *doctrina* is moreover as different from the ancient *epistēmē* as it is from the modern theory of the effective. You can clearly see that Heidegger doesn't trace meditation back through a supposed continuous and homogeneous element within a semantic history. But while taking into account the "revolutionary" (*umwälzend*) character of modern knowledge he thinks that for this modern trait (*Zug*) to appear it must be put into relation with Greek knowledge.

What then does *Wirkliches* mean, and "theory" in the sentence "(modern) science is *die Theorie des Wirklichen?*" Let's be first guided by the word *wirklich*, Heidegger proposes. The *Wirkliches* fills the domain of the *Wirkendes*, of what *wirkt*, in other words what *works* [oeuvrer] (operates, labors).[12] What does *oeuvrer* mean, not etymologically of course, etymology has conversely to be controlled and invested by "thinking" (I won't go back over that). *Oeuvrer*, *wirken* is doing (*tun*). *Tun* (before becoming "to do or make") is connected to a European root (*dhe*) from which the Greek *thesis* also derives (selective choice, intervention by Heidegger, etc.). This *tun/thesis* (placing, pose, position: *Setzung*, *Stellen*, *Lage*) is not to begin with a human activity, especially not an activity [*Tätigkeit*] in the sense of *Aktion* or *Agieren* (I quote the German because what is in *active* consideration [*ce dont* il s'agit] here—*faut*, *s'agit de*, what must be, what is in play—is not to erase what can't be gotten around in language, the effective crossing of language). So *thesis* is not at first a human activity. What happens in *physis* (upsurge, growth, power, production, etc.) is also *thesis*. Heidegger takes us back to the eve of the opposition that, as he sees it, arrives late, supervenes, that between *physis* and *thesis*, an opposition that dominates the whole of philosophy to come, from Plato on, and in fact all of philosophy [comment]. *Physis* is *thesis*: proposition (*vor-legen*), institution that causes to stand (*her-stellen*), pro-duction (*her-* and *vor-bringen*), production that brings to presence (*an-wesen*), that makes be present. Production and presentation of presence. You see that in this sense *wirken*, *tun*, *thesis-physis* designate the presentation of the present,

---

11. [Translator's Note]: Ellipsis in typescript.
12. Cf. "Science," 159 (G7, 42): "The real [*das Wirkliche*] brings to fulfillment the realm of working [*des Wirkenden*], of that which works [*wirkt*]."

production in general. *Wirkliches* (too readily translated as the real) is *Wirkendes* and *Gewirktes*, producing and product, operating and operated, what causes to be there in front of us and is there in front of us (cf. "Science," 159–60 [*G7*, 42–43]).

Another seemingly etymological trajectory is going to intersect with, enrich and complicate the previous one. The latter having just passed from *wirken* to *tun*, and from *tun* to *thesis-physis*, this one goes back from *wirken* (found in *Wirkliches*, inaccurately translated as "real," and even—I knew that when I did so but it had to be done all the same—as "effective") goes back from *wirken* to the Indo-European root *uerg*, whence *Werk* and *oeuvre* as well as *ergon* in Greek. But according to Heidegger, *ergon*, often translated as oeuvre, work, effect of efficiency, does not have its fundamental trait in *efficere* or *effectus* but in what causes to come into the unconcealed, into the appearing or the present. *Ergon* is what comes to be found and to stand in the unconcealed (*ins Unverborgene zu stehen und zu liegen kommt*). What the Greeks and especially Aristotle called *ergon*, and which the Romans translated by etymological drift as *causa efficiens*, is not the production of an effect but what is produced, what produces itself into full presence (*das ins volle Anwesen Sich-hervorbringende*).[13] That intersects with *tun-thesis-physis*. You have there the reason, and the sole reason, says Heidegger, why Aristotle calls *energeia* the presence of what is properly present (*die Anwesenheit des eigentlich Anwesenden*): "*Ergon ist das, was im eigentlichen und höchsten Sinne an-west.*"[14] All that is separated by an abyss of meaning from what came later to be designated by the modern words "energy" or "entelechy." By translating *ergon* on the basis of *operatio* understood as *actio*, in saying *actus* for *energeia*, the Romans thought, and induced us to think something quite different. And so you can well see that with this whole analysis we are at the center of the whole semantic nexus that interests us under the heading, for example, of "the practical" (*wirken*, *tun*, do, work, operate, act, etc., and there are perhaps abysses between each of those putative nuances). But the paradox is that we encounter this knot of meanings by rendering explicit not the word or concept of practice or of theory, but rather what, according to Heidegger, produces the object of modern theory in the statement "science is *die Theorie des Wirklichen*": everything resembling the practical—*wirken, tun, oeuvrer, faire, ergon, energeia, operatio,*

---

13. "a self-bringing-forth into full presencing" ("Science," 160 [*G7*, 43]).
14. "*ergon* is that which in the genuine and highest sense presences" ("Science").

actio, actus, etc.—all that is found on the side of what would be the object of modern science as theory.

Once Latin translated *energeia* as *actus*, which is not, of course, simply a linguistic or semantico-linguistic event that, following a naively idealist perspective, would draw everything along behind it (when Heidegger speaks of translation and refers to it, when he says what happens the moment the Romans translate *energeia* as *actus*, he means a relation of *Dasein* to its world as a whole, etc. [comment]), so when the Romans translate *energeia* as *operatio*,[15] what happens? The result, the product, what is given (*Ergebnis*) becomes what follows: der *Er-folg*, consequence. The *Wirkliches* (real, effective) becomes the consequence that follows what precedes, the cause; it then appears in the light of the *causa efficiens*. God himself is represented in Christian theology (which Heidegger distinguishes from faith) as *causa prima*, *Ursache*. Following hard on its heels, if you'll allow the expression, temporal succession, causality as succession, as sequence, takes the lead. That is located as much in the Kantian concept of causality as rule of succession, in the work of Heisenberg—where, Heidegger says, the causal problem is a problem of measuring time—in the definition of the real as fact (*Tat, tatsächlich*), assured and certain fact, such that *Wirkliches* comes to signify what is sure and certain, and Heidegger pursues this derivation—I'll let you read it—all the way to the value of objectivity (*Gegenständlichkeit*) that is, according to him, foreign to Greek or medieval thinking.

At this point, interrupting his analysis of the word *wirklich* in the statement "Science is the theory of the *Wirkliches*," Heidegger asks what "theory" means (cf. 163). That is where we began last time. But the strange, I would say "chiasmic" structure of how he proceeds means that in starting from one end, one extreme of the statement (on the side of the object one might say, except that, as we have just seen, the word "object" isn't adequate), starting from *wirklich*, he encounters something that isn't foreign to a certain praxis: *wirken, tun, ergon, operatio, actio, actus*, etc., and—the paradox is no less strange—starting from the other extreme, theory, science as *theōria*, he will *also* determine modern theory as a certain practice, with the result that all these semantic transformations never go further than modifying something that no doubt can't always be translated by praxis in a strict or narrow sense, but that always intersects with one of the values of praxis in general.

I won't go back over the analysis of *theōria*, we started from there last week. To conclude provisionally today I'll pick things up at the point where

15. As such in typescript.

Heidegger wants to situate what distinguishes *theōria* in Greek from modern theory or science.

Two points of reference: 1. Roman. The translation of *theōria* as *contemplatio* supposedly causes what is essential in the Greek *theōria* to disappear in one fell swoop. That translation, Heidegger goes so far as to imply, would be the origin of the sectorization, the regionalizing compartmentalization of modern science to the extent that *contemplari* means to separate, place something in a sector and enclose it there. *Templum* is from Greek *temenos*, *temein*, cut, separate (*atome*: can't be cut). *Templum* is first the sector *cut out* of the sky, and on the earth the cardinal point, the region of the sky determined by the transit of the sun. The motifs of separation, incision, cutting out, intervention that ascribes a limit, etc., in a word the inscription of the edge, all of that, named by Heidegger *einschneidendes, aufteilendes Zusehen*, had of course been partially prepared by *theōria* in Greek, but it is marked, accentuated, brought to predominance, given priority by *contemplatio* in Latin (cf. "Science," 165–66 [G7, 48]).

But also, 2nd reference point, by the German *Betrachtung*, which indeed means contemplation, vision (potentially religious, as in *vita contemplativa* opposed to *vita activa* in Christian theology), but which expresses better still what is proper to modern science, namely its interventionist activism. *Trachten* is from Latin *tractare*, which means to treat (*handeln*), elaborate; *nach etwas trachten*: to advance on or toward something by means of labor, to pursue it, elaborate it, hunt it down, set traps for it (cf. 166–67 [G7, 49]). We find here again all the semantic traits of the trait, the trace (track and trap) and tracking that we searched out—one might say cornered [*traqué*]—at the beginning of this seminar. And to follow the trace or trait is also to follow the edge. The limit of an edging is a one draught trait [*La limite d'une bordure est d'un trait*]. So, theory understood as *Betrachtung* would be that elaboration—*Bearbeitung des Wirklichen*—where we again find labor and practice on one side and the other of the statement. Doesn't that go against the essence of theory inasmuch as the latter is supposed to refrain from touching or elaborating on the real, refrain from intervening? As one says, what should be disinterested, *zweckfrei*, as pure science? Yet modern science as *Betrachtung* is indeed an elaboration, an intervening, aggressive, grabbing elaboration (*eingreifende Bearbeitung*) of the *Wirkliches*. But what Heidegger then notes in a short sentence that gives to his statement *"Die Wissenschaft ist die Theorie des Wirklichen"* all its internal coherence and its truth value as *adequatio*, is the fact that, in being an elaboration (*Bearbeitung*), modern theory or science indeed conforms to, corresponds to (*entspricht*) its object, to the very thing it elaborates, and which is, in its essence, *wirklich*, the object or effect . . . [16] of a *Wirken*, an elaborating. In this sense, and if *das Wirkliche ist das sich herausstellende Anwesende*,[17] then modern science diverts and at the same time accomplishes the Greek origin that itself diverts and accomplishes, inasmuch as the Greek philosophical origin diverted and accomplished what stood on the eve of it, as if on its edge. Diversion and accomplishment is also, on the edge, like work on the edge, a double movement of ex-propriation that diverts far from what is proper, from what is *eigen, Eigentlichkeit* and reappropriation, return (*Heimkehr*), *Besinnung* also being, necessarily, on the path to return or reappropriation. The singular logic of this ex-appropriation that distances from the *heimlich* or the *oikos* while remaining related to the *heimlich* and to the economy of the *oikos*, must be questioned, for example at the point where, as if in passing, Heidegger says that modern science is like theory in the sense of *Betrachten*—an "*unheimlich eingreifende Bearbeitung des Wirklichen*" (translate: the French translation betrays each word, but in particular *unheimlich*, by saying "an elaboration of the real, a by no means reassuring intervention in the real").[18]

What relation is there between this modern theory/practice or practice/theory and the *Unheimlichkeit*? That is what we'll slowly start to orient ourselves towards from here on. . .[19]

---

16. [Translator's Note]: Ellipsis in typescript.

17. "The real is what presences as self-exhibiting" (167, [*G*7, 49]).

18. Cf. "Science," 167 (*G*7, 49): "modern science as theory in the sense of an observing that strives after is a refining of the real that does encroach uncannily upon it."

19. [Translator's Note]: Following this ellipsis, an indented paragraph of notes appears, reading: "All that seems quite abstract—philological, linguistic, etc.—but real; elaborated; object; relation to labor, etc. Cf. Marx, Bachelard, etc. On the other hand, *unheimlich*: relation of edging to psychoanalysis."

SEVENTH SESSION

Still in order to save time, and because it would be more and more difficult, I'm giving up on going back to emphasize the links between what will follow and the six previous sessions. Let's just say, in a word, or in a sentence, that in performing "must be done" we got involved in a problematic and practice of the edge and of an overflowing of the philosophical line that we followed through all sorts of passages and reciprocal overflows, through a discourse of the Marxist philosophical type (Gramsci and Althusser) and some digressions by way of Kant, Marx ("Theses on Feuerbach"), then through Aristotle and Heidegger, each time experiencing the need to pass by way of the question of technique. While posing questions concerning Heidegger's way of proceeding and opening it to certain questions that I won't repeat, we began to read "*Wissenschaft und Besinnung*" and prepared to open "The Question Concerning Technology" (both from 1954).

Must be done. Well then, I have made a decision, that is to say also a "practical" risk, for the continuation of this Seminar and at least for this year. I am going to try to transform something in my practice, to practice differently. That will seem to affect only the form of my practice but that restriction is illusory. By desisting henceforth from referring to a previously written text—as you know that I do, notwithstanding the liberties that I take on certain occasions vis-à-vis that *prescribed* text—I am taking the risk, no doubt minimal in your eyes but quite serious in mine, and in relation to the subject and body that I am, the risk of witnessing the decomposition of both my discourse—and in a discourse there is always more or less than one discourse—and something like the authority, the credibility or the force that a prior elaboration, one that is tightly argued and calculated in advance, can confer on it. And, I would even say, however formal and minimal, rhetorical or technical that transformation might seem to you, however secondary it might seem to you, I assure you that for me it constitutes a transformation, I will almost say the most effective (*wirklich*—[comment])

transgression, the most ungovernable that there is, hence the most practical, the only one that I can think is necessary, inasmuch as it begins, for me, to transform effectively a discourse or text *on* theory/practice into another practice. Not that this discourse and the text that I was reading before this weren't practices (I think we saw that well enough), but the practice must now change and it must be done, since it's the single thing that seemed to me difficult or prohibited by my law up until now, given that my law has after all dominated this seminar from the beginning.

I can be better interrupted
we'll see how it works [*comment ça marche*]
ça marche . . . *prattein*/tra (recap)
"*Die Frage nach der Technik*"

1. the *step* [pas]
    sinnen (recap)
2. technique isn't the essence of technique
    freedom: relation of *Dasein* to essence

[Comment on 2.]
Following that preamble the first movement of the questioning meditation . . .[1] concerns the current representation of technique (*gängige Vorstellung von der Technik*),[2] the representation that has currency, the one that runs right now [*celle qui court*], goes, works, accedes or is accessible. That representation is the instrumental and anthropological representation of technique, technique as *means* in the service of an end and as human activity.

I was at that point in the preparation of this session when I noticed—no great surprise moreover—that, with its pretext of transforming further, of forging on still further, multiplying the risks and chances, my new practice of improvising on the basis of notes was not only a fiction but a mechanism that encouraged repetition—of myself or the text being commented on—an incitement to let myself be guided by the schemas already in place, the paths already forged. In short, it came down to wasted labor, that of the force of forging as well as of labor, especially when it is a matter of labor such as this. For example, while improvising I can't refer to the minute details of two texts in German, and in French translation, by Heidegger, I can't hone certain questions, work on the body of the text, or in any case I can't do that without a considerable loss that would lead us to take five

---

1. [Translator's Note]: Ellipsis in typescript.
2. Cf. "Question," 5 (*G*7, 8): "the current conception of technology."

sessions to follow the trajectory of a single one. Because it seems to me that freeing myself—at least in this situation—from the work of writing is a mystification and a simplification that goes against the very thing that we are looking for, I'll return at least provisionally to my old practice, at least at certain moments.

The current (instrumental and technological) representation of technique is a response to the question "what is technique?"

Ancient doctrine (*die alte Lehre*): the essence of a thing: what that thing is.[3]

Here double response: means in view of an end; human act; fabrication of tools, instruments, machines is a part of technique.

This representation: *exact* (richtig, correct)

Note that *instrumentum* (set of fabrication-means-ends): *Einrichtung*

Once he notes that this current representation of technique is *exact* (richtig), that is to say adequate to what one sees, what one has before one's eyes (*Richtigkeit* describes the correctness of truth as adequation of judgment to thing—cf. other texts), Heidegger specifies, by using an adjective that kept us busy last time . . .[4] that it is even *unheimlich richtig* (G7, 8), and more precisely that this *Unheimlichkeit* appears especially when one considers modern technique. Now you remember—and so we have here a systematic constant in the recourse to the word *unheimlich*—that it was "modern science" that Heidegger was calling theory, in the sense of *Betrachtung*, "*eine unheimlich eingreifende Bearbeitung des Wirklichen*" (G7, 49); and that we began to question that double motif of *Heimkehr* and the *unheimlich* in "*Wissenschaft und Besinnung*" . . . *Unheimlich* is therefore a predicate—a current one—that is regularly applied to modernity when Heidegger wants to qualify it. What does he say here? He says that the anthropological-instrumental representation of technique is exact in such an *unheimlich* way that the same goes for modern technique as well, about which one says, though—saying it also for modern science, you'll remember—that it represents something new.

Unheimlich/old/new/*Heim-kehr*/voyage/*tra-fragen*

What is *unheimlich* then is this exactness, this correctness, this pertinence of the current (instrumental-anthropological) definition of technique, and whatever difference there might be between a radar and a weather vane, a power plant and an artisanal sawmill, etc., that difference does not affect the continuity of this *Richtigkeit*.

---

3. Cf. "Question," 4 (G7, 7): "According to ancient doctrine [*nach alter Lehre*], the essence of a thing is considered to be *what* the thing is."

4. [Translator's Note]: This and the following three ellipses in typescript.

But the exact is not the true (a little different than Husserlian difference). Here also: between two determinations of truth. Everything will happen between them ...

Richtigkeit concerns technique as *mastery*, as much traditional technique as modern technique: mastery of means with a view to an end, even if it be spiritual. *Man will sie [die Technik] meistern* [comment also on the "wanting" ...].[5]

It is not just a matter of attaining mastery over nature through technique, but of attaining mastery over technique. Last week we positioned the will to know as Heidegger interprets it, saying that it is handled [*manoeuvrée*] by the other, by something other than itself. Well, here he situates the will to mastery in the relation to technique, to this metaphysical techno-logy as epoch of truth, epoch wherein truth holds itself back, is suspended (*epochē*) in its technological determination. And the will to mastery becomes all the more frustrated as technique threatens to escape human domination [*Das Meistern-wollen wird um so dringlicher, je mehr die Technik der Herrschaft des Menschen zu entgleiten droht*[6]].

Before getting involved in the movement that follows, and which is going to seek the true through the exact, with which it isn't to be confused, I would like, by developing the two questions that I posed two sessions back concerning Heidegger's way of proceeding (doesn't Heidegger reproduce philosophy, philosophy's relation to itself, in the style of questions that he poses from the edge of philosophy? I explained that question and I won't go back to it; the second, which I'll also recall in essence, consisted in asking whether, by claiming to go back through thinking, back behind metaphysics and techno-metaphysics, Heidegger doesn't reproduce this "reactive attempt" as he himself calls it in designating ["Letter on 'Humanism'"] the theoreticism that attempts to reappropriate *theōria* against practicism, etc., by going back to something more "originary," more "initial").[7] I would like, then, to develop here these two types of question that are moreover indissociable. Note first of all the complexity of the schema into which, in a discreet and almost unapparent way, Heidegger leads us. The value of *Richtigkeit* that

---

5. "We will [also: want to] master it." ("Question," 5 [*G*7, 8])

6. "The will to mastery becomes all the more urgent the more technology threatens to slip from human control." ("Question," 5 [*G*7, 8]). [Translator's Note]: Increasingly, from here to the end of the seminar, Derrida operates among paraphrase, transliteration, and translation of Heidegger's German text, making the formal distinctions between each of those practices sometimes difficult to signal.

7. "Letter on 'Humanism,'" 240.

he says goes for our instrumental and anthropological representation of technique, this *Richtigkeit* seems to define the relation of our current representation to technique: our current representation is correct, it has an accurate relation to its object. It is going to immediately become clear that the instrumental representation (*instrumentale Vorstellung*) orients, determines (*bestimmt*) the human effort in such a way that it will have an exact or correct relation to technique (*in den rechten Bezug zur Technik zu bringen*) (cf. ibid. [*G*7, 8]). The will to mastery can be read in that gesture. Now this value of *Richtigkeit* is precisely nothing other than a product or effect, if you wish, of technique, of the project of voluntarist mastery that marks the techno-metaphysical determination of truth. The determination of truth as *adequatio* (relayed from its determination as *homoiosis*) and as *Richtigkeit* precisely belongs to the techno-metaphysical epoch. Don't forget when you read *Richtigkeit* in "The Question Concerning Technology" that it's the word that Heidegger uses, in "On the Essence of Truth" for example, to name the current, derivative conception of truth as accord, suitability, adequation of a representation or utterance to what stands before, to its object (in this sense *Vorstellung*—representation inasmuch as it concerns something that is before—is condemned to this determination of truth as *Richtigkeit* [comment]). And *Richtigkeit* is even the common and invariant root of the two versions of adequation. In the first chapter of "On the Essence of Truth" (The Usual Concept of Truth) Heidegger writes:

> This dual character of the accord is brought to light by the traditional definition of truth: *veritas est adequatio rei et intellectus*. This can be taken to mean: truth is the correspondence [*Angleichung*] of the matter to knowledge. But it can also be taken as saying: truth is the correspondence of knowledge to the matter. Admittedly, the above definition is usually stated only in the formula *veritas est adequatio intellectus ad rem* [truth is the adequation of intellect to thing]. Yet truth so conceived, propositional truth, is possible only on the basis of material truth [*Sachwahrheit*], of *adequatio rei ad intellectum* [adequation of thing to intellect]. Both concepts of the essence of *veritas* have continually in view a conforming to . . . [*Sichrichten nach* . . .], and hence think truth as correctness [*rectitudo, Richtigkeit*].[8]

---

8. Martin Heidegger, "On the Essence of Truth," trans. John Sallis, in *Pathmarks*, 138. *Rectitudo* in the last bracket is Derrida's addition. Cf. Heidegger, "De l'essence de la vérité," trans. A. de Waelhans and W. Biemel, in *Questions*, vol. 1 (Paris, Gallimard, 1968), 165, Heidegger's ellipsis; "Von Wesen der Wahrheit," in *Gesamtausgabe*, vol. 9, ed. F. W. von Herrmann (Frankfurt: Vittorio Klostermann, 1976), 180.

That, then, is the *Richtigkeit* that will not be refuted, denied or contested, for all such gestures belong to the system of *Richtigkeit* (what is right is straight [*ce qui est droit est droit*], what is true in the sense of exactitude is true, exact), but its value is going to be questioned from the perspective of a more originary value of truth, as we shall see.

My question would immediately be this: does not the mode of questioning—the path of the *Fragen, Fragen* being the construction of a path in Heidegger—continue to proceed, in its very technique, in its procedure and in its processes, and to the extent that it is not purely adventurous and empirical, according to a law that remains that of techno-metaphysics and *Richtigkeit*, that is to say the system of will to mastery that cannot be dissociated from it? In constructing his path as that of a return (*Heimkehr*) toward an initial sense (*Weg zum anfänglichen Sinn*), despite all the differentiations and mutations that we took into account last time, doesn't Heidegger presume, doesn't he repeat the philosophical—here, techno-metaphysical—presumption of the semantic unity of the field, of the philosophical continuum, a continuum that clearly presumes a condition of mastery? In other words, doesn't the question concerning *Richtigkeit* submit to the very injunction of what is questioned, doesn't it repeat more or less audibly the very thing that it is questioning? Doesn't this Heideggerian type of question, seemingly posed from the edge of the philosophical, and concerning the history of philosophy as a whole, aim at ensuring mastery of a technical type over techno-metaphysics, such that it does no more than make that project develop and proliferate. And if that were so—I leave this question in the state of principle or hypothesis, without developing it—the Heideggerian text, its set of questioning procedures, its writing, its rhetorical modes, its strategies, its inscription in a technological field (in the broad sense: the political-social scene, the academic institution, the editorial machine, as well as the set of technical resources of its language—let's say its rhetoric) would also need to be analyzed, broadly and in detail, as effects of what I'll call its object, not the description or analysis or questioning of its object but the effect of its object: we have there a structure of discourse that is difficult to shape, but it seems to me necessary. Heidegger's questioning on techno-metaphysics would—according to this hypothesis—still be regulated by it.

Pause here: mastering unity (not system but . . .[9])

Reconstitute, by improvising, the problematic of the seminar: presumed semantic unity equals techno-systematic onto-encyclopedia. Against that:

---

9. [Translator's Note]: Ellipsis in typescript.

not psychoanalysis or analytic philosophy[10] (other overflowings but diffraction without unity).

Psychoanalysis: theory/practice/technique

Of Grammatology: from the first pages: link between the question of technique and the deconstruction of onto-encyclopedia and of the form of Heideggerian questioning.[11]

I now come back to the question of technique as developed in the text bearing that title. After tying the will to mastery to anthropological-instrumental representation, Heidegger makes a jump, a sudden break, to supposing that technique is not a simple means: *Gesetzt nun aber, die Technik sei kein bloßes Mittel, wie steht es dann mit dem Willen, sie zu meistern?*[12] (the will to mastering technique [is] itself will to mastery; all that refers back to will of will, out of which Heidegger is going to try to extract "freedom," like Schelling: *der nicht vollende Will*, etc., free will that no longer wills . . . see further on).[13]

What would happen, then, if technique weren't simply a means? That hypothesis is impossible if we maintain, as we are doing, that the instrumental determination—or destination (*Bestimmung*)—of technique is correct (*richtig*). It is. But, and here we have the *passage* (let's understand it at the same time as a leap and as a crossing, practical ones therefore) from one truth to another, from truth as exactness or correctness (*Richtigkeit*) to truth as unveiling of essence: correctness or exactness grasps, firmly observes (*feststellt*) what is before us (*was vorliegt*: representation of what is present), but this correct representation (of what is present before us) does not need, Heidegger makes clear, to unveil (*enthüllen*) the essence of what is present (cf. "Question," 5–6 [*G*7, 8–9]).

Unveiling of essence: freedom, not mastering will (*Gelassenheit*)

Nur dort, wo solches Enthüllen geschieht, ereignet sich das Wahre. Darum ist das bloß Richtige noch nicht das Wahre. Erst dieses bringt uns in ein freies Verhältnis zu dem, was uns aus seinem Wesen her angeht.[14]

---

10. [Translator's Note]: The French text here reads: *non pas* la *psychanalyse ou* la *philosophie analytique*, adding an emphasis that is impossible to have heard in English.

11. Cf. Derrida, *Of Grammatology*, trans. Gayatri Spivak (Baltimore: Johns Hopkins University Press, 1997), 8, 20.

12. "But suppose now that technology were no mere means, how would it stand with the will to master it?" ("Question," 5 [*G*7, 8])

13. Cf. "Question," 25 (*G*7, 26): "The essence of freedom is originally not connected with the will or even with the causality of human willing." [Translator's Note]: Ellipsis in typescript.

14. "Only at the point where such an uncovering happens does the true come to pass. For that reason the merely correct is not yet the true. Only the true brings us into a free relationship with that which concerns us from out of its essence" ("Question," 6 [*G*7, 9]).

Comment on:

- Not yet: *das bloß Richtige noch nicht das Wahre*
- "Through" twice; "approach" the true through. To approach (*in seine Nähe*) the essence of technique, one has to seek the true *durch das Richtige hindurch*.[15]

This brings us back toward the "free relationship."

The question becomes: what is instrumentality? What is the relation between a means and an end? A means is something by which something *bewirkt* and *erreicht*. What has an effect (*Wirkung*) as consequence is called *Ursache* (cause). But the end is also called cause. So where instrumentality reigns, dominates (*herrscht*), there reigns (*waltet*) causality (*Ursächlichkeit, Kausalität*).[16]

Recourse, once more, to teaching—of philosophy: "*Seit Jahrhunderten lehrt die Philosophie, es gäbe vier Ursachen.*"[17]

Read pp. 6–7, draw attention to the example (sacrifice cf. the thing, *der Krug*, jug).[18]

What is the caus*ality* of these 4 causes? Doctrine didn't fall from the sky. Until one has determined the caus*ality* of the 4 causes, causality-instrumentality-technique: *dunkel* und *grundlos*.

For a long time operating (*bewirkend*: efficient—cf. previous session—producing effects) causality has been privileged, to the extent of neglecting somewhat, even excluding the *causa finalis*.

The "doctrine of the four causes" goes back to Aristotle. But everything that we studied in Greek thinking under the rubric of Causality has nothing in common with *Wirken* and *Bewirken*.

---

15. Cf. "Question," 6 (*G7*, 9): "we must seek the true by way of the correct [*müssen wir durch das Richtige hindurch das Wahre suchen*]."

16. Cf. "Question," 6 (*G7*, 9): "A means is that whereby something is effected and thus attained. Whatever has an effect as its consequence is called a cause.... The end in keeping with which the kind of means to be used is determined is also considered a cause.... Wherever ends are pursued and means are employed, wherever instrumentality reigns, there reigns causality."

17. "For centuries philosophy has taught that there are four causes." ("Question," 6 [*G7*, 9])

18. Cf. Heidegger, "The Thing," trans. Albert Hofstader, in *Poetry, Language, Thought* (New York: Harper Collins, 2001), 161–84; "Das Ding," *Gesamtausgabe*, vol. 7, 165–87.

Ursache: (Roman) *causa*: *aition*: what *"ein anderes verschuldet"* (answers for, also in the sense of guilt, debt, etc. [comment]) (cf. "Question," 7 [*G*7, 10])

So, space of *aition* as origin of technical instrumentality, etc. (our whole problematic): space of *Verschulden* (etc.). Reminder: practice and law, transgression, debt, must be done, etc.

Strange gesture (I say "gesture": practice) of Heidegger's: seems on the basis of an example, to reconstitute in a scholarly mode Aristotle's doctrine, but by causing a lack to appear in it.

The example. Read and translate p. 8 C[19]

hylē-eidos-telos

Something odd occurs in Heidegger's text concerning the 4th cause. Read.

Heidegger doesn't give a precise reference to a text of Aristotle's. For example, if one refers to the *Metaphysics* (Book Δ (V), ch. 2, 1013) or to the *Physics* (194b ff.)[20] (a text that is literally identical and probably transposed from the *Physics* to the *Metaphysics*), the two texts where an elaboration of the 4 causes is found (and the example, among others, of the silver chalice, but without sacrifice), one is a little surprised, because of course one finds names for the first three causes (or rather the nouns *eidos* and *telos*, hence two nouns as names) but also, in addition to matter there is indeed a fourth cause (moreover Aristotle explicitly says that there are 4) and this cause is clearly stated: it is for example the sculptor in relation to the statue, and he is said to be *poioun*, or again *archē tes metaboles e staseōs e kineseōs*: of course there is no noun but there is a present participle, etc. [comment]. What does Heidegger mean that there is no word [*nom*, noun] for it?[21]

(Let's not go into the six causes in detail: particular/generic; by itself/by accident or as kind of accident; combined/simple, act/power, etc.)

Pick up again at D.

Co-responsibility (not moral or operative).

Unity of the 4: silversmith as gathering together the 3 modes.

Logos-überlegen.

Heidegger is going to rediscover *poiēsis*, which according to him isn't named by Aristotle (*poioun*, however).

---

19. [Translator's Note]: As such in typescript, appearing to refer to a notation in Derrida's copy of Heidegger, as would the "D" below.

20. Aristotle, *Basic Works*, 752–54, 240–42.

21. "The Aristotelian doctrine neither knows the cause that is named by this term nor uses a Greek word that would correspond to it" ("Question," 8).

But question of gathering as *other*. *Aition* as other, whence debt, etc. Read to p. 12. Only at that point the word *tekhnē* emerges. Technique not only means (instrumentality) but a mode of *Entbergen* (revealing).

Finish on *tekhnē* and practice: see what we said about practice as sexual practice (performance), etc.

Sexual technique and position (*thesis/physis*). Heidegger doesn't talk about that? etc.

What happens between Greek *tekhnē* and modern technique? See questions from last session.

To be continued.

EIGHTH SESSION

(Slowly)

We were interested in the question of technique as something that, far from being a simple derivation from the theory/practice opposition, would be at once the essential articulation or mediation of the opposition inasmuch as it was, according to Heidegger, the origin common to both terms. I won't go back over either Heidegger's type of questioning, or the de-limiting of that that I attempted in general terms, or even the trajectory that led us last time to a certain point in *"Die Frage nach der Technik."*

At that point the word *tekhnē* hadn't yet been pronounced.

The question concerning technique—such as it had been undertaken, with *das Fragen* forging its path, clearing by means of its path—brought out what was necessary for understanding the current representation of technique, namely the instrumental complex and the means-end relation, which meant returning toward the "primal meaning" (*anfänglicher Sinn*) of what is later called causality in order to properly (*eigentlich*) gain access to the instrumentality that inhabits causality. One of the noteworthy traits of this rereading of Aristotle's doctrine, his teaching, was the translation of *aition* by *Verschulden* (responsibility, undertaking, debt, even guilt, imputability), in short a value that installed causality—and therefore instrumentality—not in a moral or symbolic space but in the space out of which something like law could emerge, and the opposition between a so-called natural, and a non-natural (symbolic or moral) law. We'll persist in acknowledging that reading of *aition* as *Verschulden*. The second noteworthy trait of the premises of this reading is the fact that after noting that Aristotle had no noun for what is called the efficient cause (I drew your attention to the surprising idiosyncrasy of that affirmation, to tell the truth difficult to justify), Heidegger designated in the activity of the *Überlegen* by which the silversmith (*causa efficiens* of the chalice) gathered the three modes of causality—*hylē*, *eidos*, *telos*—on the basis of which the chalice obtains its first emergence (*erster Ausgang*) in terms of both appearing and entering into play in the production (*Hervorbringen*) of the chalice. If then the silversmith is co-responsible (*mitschuld*) for the chalice, his is not just any responsibility. It is responsibility for gathering the three other causalities. The gathering in the *Überlegung* (*logos*, *legein*, etc. . . .*)*[1] is neither a gesture of looking (theoretical if you wish), nor something *practical* in the sense of a manual gesture; it is the gathering condition of all that [comment]. The place of the silversmith is that of unity, of unification or rather causal gathering. So it is starting from that place that the instrumentalization of technique will come to operate (operate: all language, as you see—including the word "effect"—is caught in the effect of what takes place in the history [the gathering *Geschehen*] of *alētheia* as *tekhnē*).[2]

But curiously, just when that reading allows Heidegger to redirect the unity of the three modes or four causal co-responsibilities toward *poiēsis* (4th cause: efficient: *poioun*, let's not forget), and to emphasize the late arrival and derivativeness of the *physis*/*poiēsis* opposition, emphasizing that *physis* is even *poiēsis im höchsten Sinne* (something Heidegger seems to be saying against the apparent tradition, but . . .[3] Kant, etc.), at that moment he lets a gap appear—and we don't know whether he will in the end leave it open or close it—within the *same*ness of *physis* and *poiēsis*. That gap is the alterity of the silversmith in relation to the three other types of causality. It is in the opening of this alterity that the possibility of causal gathering will take place, and the difference, the alterity between the silversmith's cause that will be called efficient (*poioun*), and the three others, is quite simply alterity, the fact of having its cause or possibility in an other. Heidegger doesn't say that that fractures the sameness of *physis* and *poiēsis* and yet it has to be admitted that such is the possibility of every rupture or opposition between *physis* and its other or others, beginning with technique. I'll first retranslate the paragraph that concerns us, the point at which we ended last time. I'll read slowly:

> A production [*ein Hervorbringen*: we are here at the point where a thinking of production is being attempted, concerning what "to produce" will have meant, with all the consequences of that question that we can recognize], a production, *poiēsis* [Heidegger has just translated *poiēsis* in an extract from the *Symposium* as *Her-vor-bringen*] is not only artisanal fabrication [*handwerkliche Verfertigen*], it isn't only the poetic-artistic act that causes coming

1. [Translator's Note]: Ellipsis in typescript.
2. [Translator's Note]: Closing parenthesis added by translator.
3. [Translator's Note]: Ellipsis in typescript.

into appearance or into the image [*zum-Scheinen-und-ins-Bild-Bringen*]. *Physis* also [discovering itself, opening itself, blossoming on the basis of itself, *von-sich-her-aufgehen*] is also *Her-vor-bringen* [a production, *poiēsis*. In other words, nature could be called *poiēsis* and pro-duction; production is poetic and natural in that originary sense. The distinction between natural, even animal process, and human technical production, labor, if you wish, such as the whole tradition, all the way to and including Marx, will take to be assured, would come, arise out of (*survenir*) this sameness of nature and production, of *physis* and *poiēsis* as *Hervorbringen*]. *Physis* is even *poiēsis* in the highest sense [source for this evaluation? . . .[4]]. For what is present [*das Anwesende*], *physei*, has in itself [*en heautō*] *den Aufbruch des Her-vor-bringens*: [the possibility of] an opening-of-itself [a breaking into] of *pro-duction*, for example the *Aufbrechen der Blüte ins Erblühen* [comment, insist and note the *en heautō*]. *Dagegen* [on the contrary: and it's the whole reach of this on-the-contrary that will now interest us: is this on-the-contrary included in its contrary or not, etc.?], *dagegen*, what is produced as *handwerklich* und *künstlerisch*, for example the silver chalice, does not have the *Aufbruch des Her-vor-bringens* in itself but in another [*in einem anderen, en allō*], in the artisan and in the artist.[5]

Heidegger will not return to the word and value of "other" that arises here a single time in the course of his questioning, at least not in this form and thematic.

It brings to light how something like an alterity (let's not be specific, it isn't yet necessary to specify what alterity is in question here, *es handelt sich here*), something like an alterity is alone capable of gathering the 3 then 4 of causality. Is this alterity internal? Of course Heidegger doesn't say that the *en allō* is here other than nature or production, *physis* or *poiēsis*. The silversmith and his gathering *Überlegen* belongs to *physis*; but a difference opens within *physis*, within *physis* and as *physis*.

4. [Translator's Note]: Ellipsis in typescript.
5. [Translator's Note]: Here Derrida translates and parses the German text, rather than read the French translation; cf. "Question," 10–11 (*G7*, 12–13): "Not only handcraft manufacture, not only artistic and poetical bringing into appearance and concrete imagery, is a bringing-forth, *poiēsis*. *Physis* also, the arising of something from out of itself, is a bringing-forth, *poiēsis*. *Physis* is indeed *poiēsis* in the highest sense. For what presences by means of *physis* has the bursting open belonging to bringing-forth, e.g. the bursting of a blossom into bloom, in itself (*en heautōi*). In contrast, what is brought forth by the artisan or the artist, e.g. the silver chalice, has the bursting open belonging to bringing-forth not in itself, but in another (*en allōi*), in the craftsman or the artist." Greek transcriptions of *en heautō* and *en allō* in his improvised translation are his own (see discussion of, and play on those terms below).

Cryptic differance. . . .[6] [comment at length]

Heidegger leaves the *en allō* there. He doesn't talk about it anymore. But you can indeed see that it is in the difference between *en heautō* and *en allō* that the difference *physis/tekhnē* will be lodged, even if this difference belongs to nature, strangely, belongs to it strangely, like something foreign [*comme l'étranger*] . . . (*unheimlich* . . .)

Leaving there the *en allō* by which physis—I would say by means of an ellipsis that is more accurate than amusing, if you consent to go along, that physis telephones itself to itself[7]—Heidegger takes up his question on this or that side of the alternative *en heautō/en allō*: "the four causes are at play, then, within bringing-forth [production, *Her-vor-bringen*]" (11 [G7, 13]). Both what grows in nature and what the artist or artisan brings to light through his fabrication participate in production (*Her-vor-bringen*). To produce in general means in all these cases to cause to come to presence, render present. And that is where we again find the value of crypt, of a hiding-place to be unhidden, unconcealed. Inasmuch as production causes to come to presence, it causes to come out of hiding (*Verborgenheit*) into the non-hidden (*Unverborgenheit*).[8] This arrival of the hidden in the non-hidden, says Heidegger, abides and finds its impetus in what we call *das Entbergen*. The French translation, in this text, of *Entbergen* by unveiling [*dévoilement*] is insufficiently rigorous. It introduces a value of *veil*, which is elsewhere present in the word *Enthüllung* that Heidegger uses for the same movement, but here *entbergen* doesn't have recourse to the figure of the veil. It is a case of making come out (which is never without a certain force, indeed violence) from its being-hidden (*bergen*, to hide; *sich verbergen*, to save oneself, hide oneself by running off [*se cacher en se sauvant*][9] or in order to keep oneself safe).[10] *Entbergen* means to make come out of a shelter, I might say "de-lodge," not to play in a facile way by evoking the contrary of *héberger*[11] but because of the logic of *Unheimlichkeit* . . .[12] etc.

---

6. [Translator's Note]: This and the following two ellipses in typescript.

7. [Translator's Note]: *Allô* is the greeting used in French when answering the phone.

8. [Translator's Note]: The following handwritten marginal note appears here: "Not a metaphor, not for path either."

9. [Translator's Note]: *se sauver* literally means "to save oneself" but also has the colloquial sense of "taking to one's heels."

10. "The safe" appears here as a handwritten marginal addition.

11. [Translator's Note]: Derrida invents the neologism *é-berger*, pronounced the same as *héberger*, "to provide lodging," but meaning its opposite, translated therefore as "de-lodge."

12. [Translator's Note]: This and the following ellipsis in typescript.

Entbergen, Heidegger tells us, is what the Greeks called truth: *alētheia*. We Germans, he says, understand truth (*Wahrheit*) as *Richtigkeit des Vorstellens*,[13] but . . . Heidegger then feigns surprise: where have we strayed to? We are questioning concerning technique and here we have arrived at *alētheia* and at *é-bergement* without an *h*. *É-berge*, or *a-berge*, as in *alētheia*, *a-berge* is better still, it's the old word for inn [*auberge*], which comes from Germanic or High German (cf. It. *albergo*, hotel, etc.). If *physis* is still *alētheia* in its four modes of production, we haven't yet left the *auberge* or the *a-berge* despite the impression of having strayed. The figure of feigned straying, in Heidegger's pedagogical rhetoric (*Wohin haben wir uns verirrt?*) (*G7*, 13), is in harmony with the action of *Fragen* as clearing a path (practicing, *pra-tra*cking the *Weg*). But this apparent straying is already a *Heimkehr*, a path back toward the proper, toward the proper origin of technique. The fact that this proper has had to make room for a certain *en allō* by imputation is not something that holds back Heidegger's *Fragen* as such here and now. He wonders: where have we strayed to (a rhetorical question announcing that in fact we haven't strayed, and that the response that follows means "we have in fact found the most secure path," the *true*st way to the truth of technique, or better still, toward the truth of the truth of technique, the truth as production and origin of *tekhnē*). Let's read it:

> But where have we been led astray (gotten lost, *verirrt*)? We were questioning concerning technique and now we have arrived close to *alētheia*, next to *das Entbergen*. What does the essence of technique have to do with *das Entbergen*? With de-lodging? Answer: everything [*alles*]. For every producing is founded on de-lodging. Now the latter gathers within itself the four modes of causing to come forth (of causality) and rules over them [*durchwaltet*]. To its domain [*Bereich*] belong the end and means, as well as what is instrumental. The instrumental passes for the fundamental trait of technique. If we question step by step [*Schritt für Schritt*] concerning what technique represented as means properly [*eigentlich*] is, then we arrive at de-lodging [*Entbergen*]. In it resides the possibility of every productive fabrication [*herstellende Vefertigung*]. Technique, then, is not simply a means: it is a mode of *Entbergen*. If we consider it in that way, then a completely different domain for the essence of technique is opened for us. It is the domain of *die Entbergung*, that is to say of truth [*Wahr-heit*].

---

13. Cf. "Question," 12 (*G7*, 13): "We say "truth" and usually understand it as the correctness of an idea."

This perspective surprises us [literally: *befremdet uns*]. It must also do so as long as possible and in such a pressing manner that we finally take seriously the simple question of what, then, the name "technique" means.[14]

This is the first time in this text that the word, the name "technique," is considered in its own right. As if the principal aim of the whole preceding trajectory were to lead us to the point where we would be forced (by *Befremdung*) to come to a halt in front of the word, so as to pose the question: "but what does technique mean?"

Is the analysis of the word "technique"—*tekhnikon, tekhnē*—that he subsequently involves us in a semantic analysis?

Yes apparently [elaborate].

Questions already asked concerning the semantic continuum.

Is Heidegger to be reproached for questioning the word and sense, and its occurrences in a "philosophical" text (only one: *Nicomachean Ethics*, as in "*Wissenschaft und Besinnung*") and not in techno-historical "reality," etc.? Inadequacy of such an objection: what is "reality" (*Wirklichkeit*, etc.)? More efficacious question (?)[15]: presumed unity of sense: problematic as soon as what that always leads back to (presence, etc.: *physis, alētheia*) admits differance, etc., within itself.

When he posits the word *tekhnē* Heidegger proposes paying attention—as far as the *Bedeutung dieses Wortes* goes—to two things. First—this is the easiest point, so I won't dwell on it here—*tekhnē* doesn't designate only artisanal doing and capacity but that of higher art and the fine arts. *Tekhnē* is part of *poiēsis* and is something poietic (develop against the distinction

---

14. Cf. "Question," 12 (G7, 13–14): "But where have we strayed to? We are questioning concerning technology, and we have arrived at *alētheia*, at revealing. What has the essence of technology to do with revealing? The answer: everything. For every bringing-forth is grounded in revealing. Bringing-forth, indeed, gathers within itself the four modes of occasioning—causality—and rules them throughout. Within its domain belong end and means, belongs instrumentality. Instrumentality is considered to be the fundamental characteristic of technology. If we inquire, step by step, into what technology, represented as means, actually is, then we shall arrive at revealing. The possibility of all productive manufacturing lies in revealing.

Technology is therefore no mere means. Technology is a way of revealing. If we give heed to this, then another whole realm for the essence of technology will open itself up to us. It is the realm of revealing, i.e., of truth.

This prospect strikes us as strange. Indeed, it should do so as persistently as possible and with so much urgency that we will finally take seriously the simple question of what the name 'technology' means."

15. [Translator's Note]: As such in typescript.

that arrives later, between artistic or poetic and technical). And in fact the slippage from technical to poetic will appear clearly in Aristotle's text referred to by Heidegger, concerning the second point, immediately after.

This second point is more interesting. It concerns a dissociation that came about after what Heidegger calls the era of Plato, between the words *tekhnē* and *epistēmē*. Up until the era of Plato *tekhnē* was always associated with *epistēmē*. They were two names for knowledge in the broad sense. They meant the fact of knowing one's way around something or being versed in it, being good at something. Heidegger explains the link in two sentences: knowing one's way around something means that knowing it (*das Erkennen*) brings about openings (*Aufschluß*) and is therefore an *Entbergen*, a mode of *alētheuein*. Then comes the moment when *epistēmē* gets dissociated from *tekhnē*. Of course, Heidegger doesn't say Aristotle is responsible for the dissociation. It isn't brought about by a philosopher in a philosophical text, but clearly the question of the choice of reference can be asked concerning a "history" that isn't only or isn't intrinsically philosophical.

What to say about this reference itself? It is to the *Nicomachean Ethics* (Book VI, ch. 3 and 4). I'll follow it first of all the way Heidegger reads or uses it, then we'll go back and look at Aristotle's text on its own account, by means of a discussion similar to that we already had based on "*Wissenschaft und Besinnung*." I'll later tell you why.

What does Heidegger draw from this text?[16] Rather curiously—although he doesn't say as much and doesn't want to say so or recall it—that this dissociation between *tekhnē* and *epistēmē* entrenches the Aristotelian definition of *tekhnē* in the dimension of causality that, according to Heidegger, is not named by him, the dimension that has pro-duction or productive causality conversing in *allō*. So in this text Aristotle distinguishes between *tekhnē* and *epistēmē* over what they un-conceal (*entbergen*), de-lodge, and the way in which they do so. In that respect *tekhnē* is indeed, then, a mode of *alētheuein*. But—and this is what is important—*tekhnē* unconceals only what doesn't produce of itself (in itself)—based on itself—but, therefore, of the other. *Tekhnē* unconceals what doesn't pro-duce of itself and so isn't yet before us. And it does so according to the four modes of causality . . . [17] (house, ship, chalice, etc.). What is decisive in it is not, according to Heidegger, doing, manipulation, utilization of means, but *Entbergen*, etc.

But Heidegger doesn't say what separates *tekhnē* from *epistēmē*; not *en allō*. He says that production produces something that wasn't there before

16. An illegible handwritten marginal addition appears here.
17. Ellipsis in typescript.

and that can take this or that form. He leaves all the rest of Aristotle's text in the shadows in order to insist on *tekhnē* as pro-duction and as *Entbergen*, as *alētheuein*.

We are going to take a detour through this text by Aristotle, at least because it includes a definition of the *praxical* in its relation to the *technical*, a definition that in itself matters to us in this seminar, but also because it is totally absent, in name at least, from the text by Heidegger that we are reading right now. That fact is all the more strange given that this notion of praxis is at the heart of the text referred to by Heidegger.

The passage from Aristotle follows precisely the one we analyzed several weeks ago (*Nicomachean Ethics* VI 3 1139b15). From the outset one is indeed struck by the fact that *tekhnē* is quite explicitly included, as Heidegger says, among the modes of *alētheuein*, or more precisely among the means by which the soul (*psychē*) tells what is true in an affirmative or negative way (*kataphanai ē apophanai*). There are five such means: the first to be named is *tekhnē*, then comes *epistēmē*, then *phronēsis* (generally translated as prudence), then *sophia* (wisdom), and *nous* (intuitive reason).

Aristotle begins by defining science (*epistēmē*): the relation to necessary things, things that can't be otherwise than they are (eternal, unengendered, incorruptible). He then goes on to things that can be otherwise than they are (*allōs*)....[18] These things that can be otherwise than they are first put into two categories, those that are the effect of *poiēsis* and those that are the effect of *praxis*, *poieton* and *prakton*. *Poiēsis* isn't *praxis* (production/action according to the French translation), and one isn't a part of the other, neither *hexis* vis-à-vis *poiēsis* nor *hexis* vis-à-vis *praxis*. For example, architecture is a form of *tekhnē* and a "capacity to make,"[19] to produce (*poiein*) according to a *logos* (rule), and there is no *tekhnē* (no art, if you wish) that isn't a readiness to produce (*poiein*) according to a *logos*. There is then an identity, Aristotle says, between *tekhnē* and readiness to *poiēsis* according to a *logos*, between *tekhnē* and *poiēsis* (according to a *logos*). *Tekhnē* is always a matter of becoming (*genesis*) and applying oneself to *tekhnē* means considering (*theōrein*, technique is inseparable from *theōria* here) how to bring to existence things that can be or not be but whose principle (*arkhē*) of existence is in what is *poioun* and not in the poem (in the artist and not in the produced poetic thing, in the producer and not in the product: different from "nature": *oute tōn kata physis*: root of the opposition *tekhnē/physis*). It follows that just as *praxis* and *poiēsis* are different, so *tekhnē* forms part of *poiēsis* and not *praxis*;

---

18. [Translator's Note]: Ellipsis in typescript.
19. Aristotle, *Basic Works*, 1025.

closer to *theōria* than to *praxis*. Certainly, what emerges from that is indeed what we said about practical intellect and theoretical intellect in our reading of the previous passage from the *Nicomachean Ethics*—namely that despite the hierarchy that puts the theoretical above the practical, they have one and the other an essential link with *logos* and with truth—well we can now also say that about *tekhnē*, which always produces according to a *logos* and is therefore foreign to animality.

What now of the distinction that is maintained so clearly, and with such insistence by Aristotle between *tekhnē* (which is *poiēsis*) and *praxis* (which is translated as action, and covers the domain of moral and political action, of conduct, etc.)? Always below technical life <illegible reference>.[20]

How does the at least apparently modern category of labor that is readily associated with that of practice get situated in this schema? It appears closer to *tekhnē* than to Aristotelian *praxis*.[21] And yet, to the extent that thinking, let's say modern thinking concerning labor, has at least this as a constant and invariant (as much in Hegel as in Marx and whatever their oppositions may be in that regard), it has this as a constant, that it no longer dissociates *tekhnē* from *praxis*, namely from labor in its productive scope and its sociopolitical inscription, *praxis* in the Aristotelian sense of political action, conduct of man in society. *Tekhnē* and *praxis* cannot be separated, even de jure, in a modern concept of labor, in the way that they are separated in Aristotle and finally in Heidegger, who maintains the separation. Moreover it can be asked—I'll here just pose a difficult question to which I am far from possessing the answer—whether the concept of labor is translatable in Greek, or rather whether it translates something whose conceptual unity is thinkable in Greek philosophy, whether this doesn't point to an example of a discontinuous process, of an irreducible emergence, irreducible to a semantic continuity and to the style of question or hermeneutics that it calls for. Even when Heidegger speaks of labor—elsewhere than in "The Question Concerning Technology"—in order to say, as you know, precisely that labor constitutes the essential determination of being according to modern materialism, even at that moment, for obvious reasons he ties labor to *tekhnē* and not to *praxis*, which allows him to bring back modern materialism to the history of a metaphysics, of the metaphysics that brings *tekhnē* back to *alētheia*, etc.

20. The preceding phrase is a barely legible handwritten addition.

21. The following sentence, which has been typed, then struck out by hand in the typescript, appears here: "We'll take up these questions next time: question of 'technical' modernity in Heidegger, read Lacoue-Labarthe." See subsequent references.

Comment at length.
Read "Letter on 'Humanism,'" p. 259:

> The essence of materialism does not consist in the assertion that everything is simply matter but rather in a metaphysical determination according to which every being appears as the material of labor. The modern metaphysical essence of labor is anticipated in Hegel's *Phenomenology of Spirit* as the self-establishing process of unconditioned production, which is the objectification of the actual through the human being, experienced as subjectivity. The essence of materialism is concealed in the essence of technology, about which much has been written but little has been thought. Technology is in its essence a destiny within the history of being and of the truth of being, a truth that lies in oblivion. For technology does not go back to the τέχνη of the Greeks in name only but derives historically and essentially from τέχνη as a mode of ἀληθεύειν, a mode, that is, of rendering beings manifest.[22]

You will say: but if he had brought labor back to Aristotelian *praxis* the result would have been the same. Yes, but perhaps not so if he were to have broken the dissociation between *tekhnē* and *praxis* effected by Aristotle and if new concept, new organization, etc.

Instead of making that type of gesture, what does Heidegger do? He doesn't, as we have already seen, seek to erase every modern transformation of *tekhnē*, of the historial experience of *tekhnē*. But that modern transformation remains, I'll say, under the sway [*coup*] of initial and more than initial truth.

Heidegger poses the question: what is modern technique? For if technique is a mode of *Entbergen*, if it is deployed wherever truth comes about (*geschieht*), has its place, one can ask whether that also goes for modern technique and not only for the artisanal technique of the Greeks. It is said: modern technique presupposes exact science of nature, but reciprocally, and stating this doesn't get us any further. . . .[23] One therefore must know what modern technique is, all the more so because it is from the latter that the "unsettling" element (*das Beunruhigende*) comes to us.

From there on read and comment . . .

---

22. [Translator's Note]: Derrida's typescript note to himself is to read pp. 103–5 of the French edition, corresponding to 259–60 in the English translation quoted here.

23. [Translator's Note]: This and the following ellipsis in typescript.

NINTH SESSION

Now I would like, without artifice, without too much rhetorical artifice (but every rhetorical artifice can be evaluated and, to begin with, analyzed, only on the basis of the question concerning technique and even concerning psychoanalytical technique), I would now like without too much artifice to link my reading of Heidegger, of the last part of "The Question Concerning Technology," to the discussion that we have just had.[1] That discussion brought out at least this much, to remain at the level of what is minimal and incontestable: the history of the analytical movement, of the analytical society (its internal conflicts, its institutional regulations, its inscription in the sociopolitical field, which is not simply that of a part within a whole but obeys a more complex logic, as we've seen, etc., etc.), this history of the analytical society—in spite of its youth and novelty (three quarters of a century) it is not simply a fragment within a broader history but has relations with that history that are not those of a part to a whole, because, as concerns also the notion of society, it claims to rethink the category and logic of historicity—that history and problematic of the analytical society plays, and is called to play in so-called Western society a role that, in the first place, can no longer be considered regional, circumscribed, confined. That history of the analytical society, of analytical societies—and the war and wars that rage and will continue to rage among them—is only just beginning, it will have involved no more than two or three generations. But without even drawing up the list of all the frontiers that are implicated in that history and in the conflictual situation of the analytical society, of analytical societies (the politico-analytical field, the so-called theoretical field, the theoretico-didactic field—the university—the onto-encyclopedic field, the medical field, all of

---

1. The exact program for the teaching year could not be reconstituted. Certain allusions lead one to believe that some sessions were devoted to student presentations and discussions, of which no written trace remains.

them artificial distinctions that I mention only briefly), without even drawing up the list of all those frontiers, it suffices in principle to keep in mind the fact that the psychoanalytical project does not claim simply to be the consequence or application, the "regionalization" of schemas relating to the theoretical, knowledge or truth, the practical, the technical, etc., but offers itself as transformation, displacement and re-elaboration of everything that we call by those names, and including the name "name" [*jusqu'au nom de nom*]. That is enough to recognize that the question of the analytical institution isn't a <illegible> question.[2]

Given that—and this is the movement announced at the beginning of this seminar on Theory/Practice—a new departure must be made on the basis of the following evidence: psychoanalysis speaks of theory, of practice, of analytical technique but claims to modify each of those concepts and especially the relation between each of those concepts. In psychoanalysis the theoretical is given as something indissociable from the practical, but psychoanalytical practice in particular is given as irreducible to anything else whatsoever that can be designated by the name of *practice*. It is a practice within which, if one refers to a common sense of practice, doing, the act, one does nothing, one doesn't act, one certainly doesn't act out (in word, and "labor," transference). And yet, it is not simply as a simple paleonymic convention that one calls that "practice," and what takes place or gets done there could indeed claim to lead us back to the most hidden sense of the practical (cf. Aristotle, desire and logos, etc., and even back before Aristotle). Above all, passing very quickly over the immense problems whose surface I have just barely skimmed, I would like, in order to link things, to insist on the question of analytical technique, of the analytical sense of technique in that practice. What welds analytical theory to so-called analytical practice, what defines the site of their indissoluble, I would say unanalyzable articulation, is what is called analytical "technique." The question of "analytical technique" is not a subsidiary question to the grand theoretical and practical questions of psychoanalysis. It governs the relation between the two and it is indeed at that site of mediation, of articulation between theoretical and practical that the whole stakes of the analytical movement, and of the agonistic relations within the analytical society are situated. Apparently, analytical technique, the instituted rules concerning analytical technique form what is most *thetic*, what is most institutional within the institution: they are the rules instituted by the *nomothete*, by the founding

---

2. This sentence reconstitutes a barely legible marginal addition. [Translator's Note]: The illegible word might be "practical" or "limited to itself [*particulière*]."

father, at least by him who was, and had himself recognized as such at the origins of the analytical society, origins whose history still remains to be analyzed in detail, with all the paradoxes that such a project might conceal; instituted then by him who had himself recognized by positing not only the rules of analytical technique but the very processes and institution of his own recognition. One has there an event of self-institution, auto-thesis, of the auto-*thete* or auto-*tely* whose enigma relates in the first place to the idea that the auto- cannot come to a halt, start moving, set out, determine its economy (parking, savings, tradition) except by soliciting in a strange way what relates via *allō* (including responsibility, *verschulden*, and transfer of responsibility), removing the limit separating *en heautō* and *en allō*. I leave aside for the moment the enormous problem of this auto-hetero-institution in order to mark the point that matters to me here, namely that the rules of technique, rules that imply theoretical knowledge, a new conceptuality (concerning knowledge of what the unconscious, language, transference, etc. is), but that also define the conditions of a new practice, those technical rules, which form the cornerstone of the analytical institution have no doubt been instituted by the *nomothete* on the basis of what he considered to be practical experience and theoretical knowledge. But since very quickly, as close as possible to the source, that practical experience and theoretical knowledge were themselves conditioned by the structure of a technique on the way to becoming an institution and right in the middle of forging that path [*en plein frayage*] the whole problem of what founds, legitimizes, authorizes the institution of such rules, rules that have also provided the protocols of experience—practical and theoretical protocols—that whole problem remains intact. There is a circle there, which is neither the Hegelian nor the hermeneutic circle (Heideggerian, for example), but an original circle that calls for a new problematic. Those technical rules appear to be simple, small in number and very stable: standard treatment (transference, free association, saying everything, doing nothing, couch—body, etc.).[3] It appears, more than any theoretical discourse, more than any empirical practice, to be the simple untouchable charter, the unchangeable, almost sacred constitution of the analytical society. As with every constitution, this one belongs to a language that acts more than states or describes, that institutes and produces, that performs if you wish. The institution of those rules is already a language that posits, operates, engages, and this "practical" character of the technical institution already poses the problem of a practice that is older than the practice,

---

3. [Translator's Note]: The fragment that follows the colon reconstitutes a partially legible handwritten marginal insertion.

than what the *nomothecy* establishes: it is a practical language (a "performative"), if you wish, that act, posits and inaugurates the conditions of a practice. That instituting practice is in a "transcendental" position, if you wish, in relation to the practice that it makes possible, even though Freud claimed to draw the consequences of his theory and practice on the spur of the moment. But the performative that does something by saying what must be (the rule) isn't a performative in the strict sense or like any other, presuming at least that there were such a thing as a performative in the strict sense: it doesn't conform to a context of existing conventions as does the performative according to Austin; or at least, since in spite of everything all sorts of existing conventions and contracts intervene in the conditions of possibility of the instituting [*instauration*] of psychoanalytic technique, let's say that at a certain point that instituting claims to create absolutely its own conventionality, its own irreducible contractuality, one that is irreducibly heterogeneous to ambient conventionality [comment, discuss]. This charter that, by means of an act of language, a language-act, an act, produces a set of minimal rules, a very simple corpus of absolutely original rules, this charter seems untouchable. And in fact whoever interferes with it seems to require—as though one were sacrilegious or a criminal, outside of society—exclusion or excommunication from the society. But we know that that simple untouchability is neither simple nor untouchable, that through the question of transference (cf. last week) it opens—based on that model—the limits of the enclosure of the treatment; and especially that the question of psychoanalytic teaching, of the training of analysts by means of a standard treatment that cannot simply be closed upon itself, immediately opens analytical practice to the field that I call textual in the general sense, edgeless, the question of training, then, as question of theoretico-practical technique becomes the stakes of a war and incessant movement that is far from being closed, that is today entering a phase—we have all sorts of indications of this—that is more critical and more unpredictable than ever (we'll talk more about it).

It wasn't my intent today to get deep into this problem or these problems (we'll come back to them next week with Chalenset's presentation).[4] I want just to identify these points of reference to pose the question:

Is psychoanalytic technique, problematized thus, is psychoanalytic technique, the technique that is the first, and only one to regulate its institution on something—if it can still be said—like the unconscious, is this technique

---

4. Unidentified participant.

a modern technique? Wait for me to go a little further before taking on this question that will seem to you a little strange, if not a little stupid.

When I say "modern technique" I have in view what Heidegger calls by that name when, in his *Besinnung* on the question of technique, he proposes getting to the era of modern technique following the passage that we read together a few weeks ago. Does psychoanalytic technique, about which Heidegger obviously doesn't say a word, which he is no doubt far from thinking about (even though in *"Wissenschaft und Besinnung"* he speaks of psychiatry in the context of modern science), does psychoanalytic technique belong to the era that Heidegger determines—we'll see how—as that of modern technique? How is it situated in relation to this modern technique? Is it situated, does it allow itself to be situated by it, by what Heidegger calls modern technique? Or, on the contrary, does it overflow the limits, indeed overflow conceptuality and *Fragestellung* itself? Can Heideggerian *Fragestellung* take into account something like psychoanalytic technique (for example its *allō*), or rather is it designed to exclude it, to foreclose it, etc.? But what is an exclusion, in a text? [Elaborate]

Starting from there return to Heidegger's text; underscore again *en allō* (other in nature? other origin—ego transcendental or otherwise? unconscious? the unconscious for Heidegger, era of consciousness . . .[5])

We ended last time at the point where Heidegger, having deployed the schema you are familiar with, concerning *tekhnē* as pro-duction and as mode of *Entbergen* or of *alētheuein*, poses the question "what is modern technique?," the only question whose disturbing (*beunruhigen*) form impels us to ask what technique is. We saw how he began to respond to that question. Modern technique is also an *Entbergen* (from this point of view psychoanalysis also; an *Entbergen* not tied to consciousness or representation) and it is only by taking into account the essential continuity of this fundamental trait that one gains access to what is new in modern technique. Its novelty is that *Entbergen* is no longer deployed via a pro-duction (*Her-vor-bringen*) in the sense of *poiēsis* (you will remember) but as *Heraus-fordern* (pro-vocation) that grabs, requires, violently extracts and accumulates (psychoanalysis?). We followed the analysis of that violent, extracting exploitation, of that *Bestellung* that *commits* and *summons* (stellt) nature, the field, the river, the mine to deliver, furnish, exhibit, one might almost say own up to what it has in its belly.

That belly is something to which Heidegger gives the status of a standing-reserve [*fonds*] (*Bestand*); what is committed to its *Stand*, its position and

---

5. [Translator's Note]: Ellipsis in typescript.

stability. Heidegger calls this stable position a *Bestand*, which means more than a stock or reserve (*Vorrat*). The fund is not yet an object (*Gegenstand*)....[6]

In relation to that fund, what interpellates in a provocative way and de-lodges the fund as real is apparently the human. But although man himself in his apparent activity seems to be the subject of this persecuting provocation he is himself *heraus-gefordert* (challenged, committed, mandated, asked, interpellated) from the position of what—the other—attracts him, bears him toward the non-hidden, the de-lodged, the *Unverborgenes*. By uncovering, de-lodging, man responds to this *Zuspruch der Unverborgenheit*. "Thus modern technique *als das bestellende Entbergen* [de-lodging that commits, that undertakes a commission] is not a simply human *Tun* [bottom of p. 26 of the German text]."[7] Man is constituted, gathered in this provoking commission. How to name what gathers man in this way? Heidegger has recourse to the gathering *Ge-* that is in effect in *Gebirg* [*Berge*] or *Gemüt* [*zumute ist*] and names *Ge-stell* the gathering that provokes and gathers man by calling him, interpellating him to commit as fund what de-lodges itself.[8]

Arbitrary, bizarre choice? Cf. example of Plato's use of *eidos* ("Question," 20 [*G7*, 21]). Path-clearing practice language.

The *Ge-stell* that governs the essence of modern technique is not in itself technical.

Ge-stell (taking over [*arraisonnement*] . . .) as provocation retains a relation to *stellen*, *her-stellen* and *dar-stellen* (place upright, out in front, make and expose: erection [statue]). In this *Ge-stell* there is produced (*ereignet sich*) the *Unverborgenheit* in conformity with which the labor of modern technique de-conceals, de-lodges the real (*Wirkliches*) as fund. But this de-concealing, this un-crypting (bringing out of its hiding place) is neither a human act nor a means, an instrument in the service of man.[9]

---

6. [Translator's Note]: Ellipsis in typescript. This and three subsequent ellipses, which appear as such in the typescript between here and the end of the seminar, perhaps indicate Derrida's intention to provide further commentary.

7. Cf. "Question," 19 (*G7*, 20): "Modern technology as an ordering revealing is, then, no merely human doing."

8. [Translator's Note]: For *Ge-stell* the English translation has "Enframing" (cf. "Question," 19 [*G7*, 20]).

9. Cf. "Question," 21 (*G7*, 22): "In Enframing, that unconcealment comes to pass in conformity with which the work of modern technology reveals the real as standing-reserve. This work is therefore neither only a human activity nor a mere means within such activity."

The instrumental conception that we spoke of at length at the beginning of this reading becomes completely obsolete.

Ge-stell: *Schicken*: *Ge-schick*: freedom (not subordinated to will, to the causality of human wanting).

Freedom: joined by the closest relation to truth as movement of a veil: "Freedom is what hides by lighting up *das lichtend Verbergende* and in whose clearing [*Lichtung*] there floats the veil [*Schleier*] that veils [*verhüllt*] *das Wesende aller Wahrheit* and causes the veil to appear as what hides [veil: *den Schleier als den verhüllenden erscheinen läßt*]."[10]

(Double Session and question of style . . .)[11]

Relation to psychoanalysis: can it shed light on this veil or the opposite? [comment at length].

In the free element (in the sense of destiny) relation to the essence of technique can be:

- neither constraint charging headlong toward technique
- nor fleeing as though from a *Teufelswerk* (relation to the demonic in *Beyond the Pleasure Principle*: last year).[12]

No devil but *Gefahr*: modern technique neither dangerous nor demonic (*es gibt keine Dämonie*) but *Geheimnis ihres Wesens*.

"We think *Ge-stell* in the sense of *Geschick* and *Gefahr*."[13]

What is the threat of this danger that properly belongs to the destiny of freedom? What is the danger of *Ge-stell* inasmuch as it is and hides the essence of modern technique?

This danger, this threat doesn't come from machines or apparatuses, in other words from technical things. The threat comes from the essence

---

10. Cf. "Question," 25 (*G7*, 26): "Freedom is that which conceals in a way that opens to light, in whose clearing there shimmers that veil that covers what comes to presence of all truth and lets the veil appear as what veils."

11. Cf. Derrida, "The Double Session" in *Dissemination*, trans. Barbara Johnson (Chicago: University of Chicago Press, 1981); *Spurs: Nietzsche's Styles / Éperons: les Styles de Nietzsche*, trans. Barbara Harlow (Chicago: University of Chicago Press, 1979).

12. Cf. Derrida, "To Speculate—on 'Freud,'" in *The Post Card*, trans. Alan Bass (Chicago: University of Chicago Press, 1987). That text was presented as part of the previous year's "Life Death" seminar. The initials "SK" follow the reference to last year, perhaps referring to either Sarah Kofman or Søren Kierkegaard.

13. Cf. "Question," 28 (*G7*, 29): ". . . we think Enframing in the sense of destining and danger."

of technique, from *Ge-stell* ("co-erecting" taking over?): co-erection: correction: I propose translating *Ge-stell* as *correction*: not what gathers a double-banding but gathers erection (*Aufstellung*) in itself, etc. Cf. Lacoue-Labarthe.[14]

The threat comes from correction inasmuch as it threatens man's being. The threat proper (*die eigentliche Bedrohung*) comes from the *Ge-stell* (correction) that the mastery of *Ge-stell* (*Herrschaft des Ge-stells*) threatens with the possibility that coming back to a more originary de-lodging is refused (*daß des Menschen versagt sein könnte, in ein ursprünglicheres Entbergen einzukehren*), along with experiencing and understanding thus the call (*Zuspruch*) of a more initial truth (*eine anfänglichere Wahrheit zu erfahren*).[15]

Comment at length. Why I translated *Ent-bergen* by de-lodging [*é-bergement*] (return: *einkehren*). Correction (*Ge-stell*) threatens the return to more original un-veiling.

Relation to psychoanalysis . . . [comment].

Danger: the safe [*le sauf*], salvation [*salut*] (every man for himself [*sauve qui peut*])

> "*Wo aber Gefahr ist,*
> *wächst Das Rettende auch*" (Hölderlin)

What does safe, "to save" mean? Usually we think that "to save" means to seize in time something threatened with destruction, and to put it securely in its previous *Fortbestehen*. But "*retten*" means, besides that: to conduct (*einholen*: go to meet, go get) *ins Wesen*, in its essence, in order to bring that essence into its proper appearing (*um so das Wesen erst zu seinem eigentlichen Scheinen zu bringen*).[16]

---

14. Philippe Lacoue-Labarthe, "Typography," in *Typography*, ed. Christopher Fynsk (Stanford, CA: Stanford University Press, 1998). [Translator's note]: See also Derrida, *Glas*, trans. John P. Leavey and Richard Rand (Lincoln: University of Nebraska Press, 1990).

15. Cf. "Question," 28 (*G7*, 29): "The threat to man does not come in the first instance from the potentially lethal machines and apparatus of technology. The actual threat has already affected man in his essence. The rule of Enframing threatens man with the possibility that it could be denied to him to enter into a more original revealing and hence to experience the call of a more primal truth."

16. Cf. "Question," 28 (*G7*, 29): "Thus, where Enframing reigns, there is *danger* in the highest sense:

> *But where danger is, grows*
> *The saving power also.*

I insist on "proper," the proper appearing of the essence: safe: proper: safe conduct toward the proper, etc.

Comment at length (relation to psychoanalysis) with rest of text in hand (underlined passages).

Let us think carefully about these words of Hölderlin. What does it mean 'to save'? Usually we think that it means only to seize hold of a thing threatened by ruin, in order to secure it in its former continuance. But the verb 'to save' says more. 'To save' is to fetch something home into its essence, in order to bring the essence for the first time into its genuine appearing."

INDEX OF NAMES

Aeschines (of Athens), 31
Althusser, Louis, 9n12, 16, 21–23, 32, 37, 39–40, 42–52, 53–59, 61–67, 69–74, 88n10, 97
Angelus Silesius, 27
Aristotle, 10, 30, 47, 76, 80–82, 84–85, 92, 97, 104–5, 107, 113–16
Austin, J. L., 6, 120

Bachelard, Gaston, 48–49, 95n19
Bernstein, Eduard, 57
Brisset, Jean-Pierre, 37–38

Comte, Auguste, 46
Croce, Benedetto, 14–15, 21, 39, 44

Engels, Friedrich, 9, 22, 23, 57, 70, 72

Feuerbach, Ludwig, 8–10, 12–17, 21, 22, 32, 35, 40, 49, 74
Freud, Sigmund, ("founding father [of psychoanalysis]", 118–20

Goethe, Johann Wolfgang von, 27
Gramsci, Antonio, 14–16, 21, 39, 44, 53, 70, 97

Hegel, G. W. F., 10, 14, 31, 37, 47, 54, 60, 61, 73, 81, 115, 116, 119
Heidegger, Martin, 4n4, 17, 26–27, 59–61, 72–117, 121–25
Heisenberg, Werner, 93

Hölderlin, Friedrich, 79, 124
Husserl, Edmund, 23, 36–37, 47, 60, 85, 88, 100

Jacob, François, 38n31

Kant, Immanuel, 10, 23–28, 30, 31n21, 32–37, 41, 45, 47, 60, 73, 82, 84, 88, 93, 97, 108
Kierkegaard, Søren, 123
Kofman, Sarah, 123
Korsch, Karl, 45

Lacoue-Labarthe, Philippe, 124
Leibniz, Gottfried Wilhelm, 27
Lenin, Vladimir, 45, 55–57, 70, 72
Lévi-Strauss, Claude, 72
Louis IX (Saint-Louis), 42
Lukács, György, 45

Mao, Zedong, 56
Martin, Jacques, 49
Marx, Karl, 5, 7–17, 21–24, 26, 31, 32, 35, 36–37, 38n31, 39–67, 69–75, 84, 88n10, 95n19, 97, 109, 115

Nietzsche, Friedrich, 60, 72

Pierssens, Michel, 38
Plato, 10, 30, 47, 76, 80, 81, 91, 113, 122
Ponge, Francis, 29

Sartre, Jean-Paul, 60
Stalin, Joseph, 44

www.ingramcontent.com/pod-product-compliance
Lightning Source LLC
Chambersburg PA
CBHW022018290426
44109CB00015B/1215